The Art of Teaching Craft

A COMPLETE HANDBOOK

JOYCE SPENCER AND DEBORAH KNEEN

SALLY MILNER PUBLISHING

First published in 1993 by
Sally milner Publishing Pty Ltd
at 'The Pines'
RMB 54 Burra Road
Burra Creek NSW 2620
Australia

Reprinted 1993, 1994, 1995, 1996

© Deborah Kneen & Joyce Spencer, 1993

Design by Gatya Kelly, Doric Order
Illustrations by Deborah Kneen
Cover photograph by Rodney Weidland
Typeset in Australia by Asset Typesetting Pty Ltd
Printed in Australia by Impact Printing, Melbourne

National Library of Australia
Cataloguing-in-Publication data:

Spencer, Joyce.
   The art of teaching craft.

   ISBN 1 86351 106 7

   1.Handicraft — Study and teaching. I. Kneen,
   Deborah.
   II. Title.(Series : Milner craft series).

745.507

ACKNOWLEDGEMENTS

Thank you to the many people who contributed to our book:

Our husbands, Peter Kneen and Geoff Spencer.

The teachers who submitted lesson plans and notes: Denise Ferris, Laurel Lawson, Vivian Orrell, Sharon Wilkes.

Those who supplied valuable ideas and comments: Joan Alenson, Judy Allen, the Australian Copyright Council, Diana Brandt, Jennifer and Graeme Bowe, Gloria Circosta, June Cooper, Elizabeth Dunne, Monica Hall, Robyn Harvey, Phyll Hill, Pamela Jones, Suzanne Kelly, Janet Klepatzki, Peter Kneen, Nitsa Kyriacou, Denise Lawler, Mary McCullah, Suzie Roberts, Margaret Shipley, Nerida Singleton and many anonymous contributors.

The art and craft teachers who attended our Effective Teaching seminars and whose positive response and support prompted us to write this book. We have been delighted to hear back from them that they have successfully applied the techniques learnt in the seminar to their own teaching situations.

Sally Milner and her team for their enthusiastic support of this project and Rodney Weidland for the beautiful cover photography.

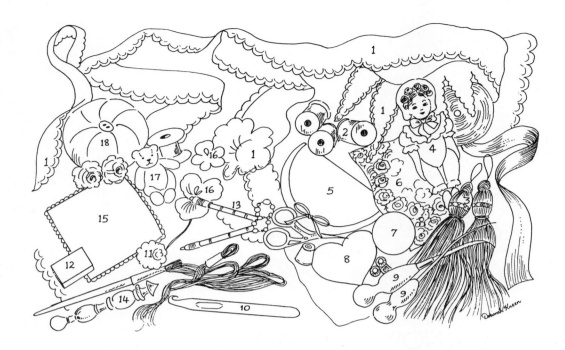

COVER CREDITS

FRONT COVER

1 Antique laces
2 Old silks
3 Silk tassels, c. 1920; 1, 2 and 3, courtesy of Joanne Hill
4 Painted bisque jointed doll, courtesy of Phyll Hill
5 Crazy patchwork chatelaine, by Denise Lawler of Cottage Crafts at Camden Park
6 Silk ribbon embroidery on velvet by Joyce Spencer
7 Découpage brooch by Nerida Singleton
8 Folk art painted heart by Deborah Kneen
9 Antique leather-working tools

BACK COVER

10 Large chain crochet hook; 9 and 10, courtesy of Joyce Spencer
11 Porcelain rose brooch
12 Petit point pill box; 11 and 12, courtesy of Elly Kriz
13 Antique lace bobbins, courtesy of Joan Alenson
14 Turned wooden needlecase
15 Antique cross-stitched lavender sachet; 14 and 15, courtesy of Joanne Hill
16 Old hand-made velvet flowers, courtesy of Elaine Schmidt
17 Miniature felt bear, courtesy of Deborah Kneen
18 Pin cushion by Elizabeth Adair

CONTENTS

INTRODUCTION

The desire to make articles had its origins in early man's most practical needs. For instance, baskets as containers needed to be light yet strong, created quickly from leaves or bark and tied with vine. Fur was roughly joined or stitched to make warm clothing. Jewellery was made from pebbles, shells, even bones and teeth. These craft skills were passed from one generation to the next in a natural learning process. It is amazing how often primitive cultures created the most amazing artefacts. Only now are we understanding how inventive and imaginative they were.

Today, we use crafts as therapeutic and recreational activities or as a means of self expression, to create and achieve something special with our own hands. Whether it's folk art, needlecraft, calligraphy, or découpage, all crafts require expert teachers.

WHY TEACH?

Contemporary craftspeople teach for many reasons. Sometimes they do so on a voluntary basis, without remuneration and for the personal satisfaction of sharing their gift with others. Some teachers have been coaxed into it by a friend or organisation. Many teach on a part-time basis, often as a means of 'feeding' their craft habit: of providing the funds to purchase books and equipment and to attend craft classes and workshops. However, an increasing number of craftspeople find that, through either choice or economic necessity, teaching has become their main occupation and source of income.

TEACHING CONDITIONS

Craft teachers today need to be innovative, informed and adaptable. Classes can be held in a variety of places: churches, private homes, hospitals, nursing homes, clubs, schools, shops and even outdoors.

Not all these settings constitute ideal teaching environments. Whether you teach in a well-equipped studio or around the kitchen table, the responsibility is yours to maintain a high teaching standard and to share your skills with enthusiasm. If you are not enthusiastic, you cannot then expect your students to be!

TEACHING SKILLS

How does one become a good teacher? A gifted few possess innate teaching ability, a natural skill with which they are born. For most people, good teaching technique comes with training and experience.

Craft teachers in primary and high schools and the TAFE system generally have some formal training in teaching methodology, as well as access to on-going in-service courses. But the majority of craft teachers, working in shops, evening colleges and at the community level, are thrown in at the deep end, without guidance or training.

The good craftsperson will be in great demand as a teacher, but that does not necessarily mean he or she will be able to teach effectively. You may know of an artisan who is outstanding in that field, but he or she just cannot put the message across in the classroom. Students leave the class feeling frustrated and even cheated because they have expected so much and then have learnt so little.

These, then, are the two extremes of craft teaching: the crafter who is a born communicator, and the brilliant artisan who doesn't know how to share that knowledge. As crafters and teachers, most of us fall somewhere in between. You need, of course, to be competent in your craft and to be secure in your knowledge and ability. It is not necessary, however, to be a magnificent craftsperson in order to be a good craft teacher.

TRAINING THE TRAINER

To date, teachers of craft have been offered little comprehensive guidance as to how to be better teachers. There is an abundance of material showing how to *do* crafts but very little on how to *teach* them. This handbook aims to fill that gap, by showing you how to communicate your craft skills in a clear, pleasant and positive way.

In researching this book, comments have been sought from expert craft teachers in many fields about the factors which determine successful teaching. In addition, a wide sample of students were canvassed about their expectations of craft courses and teachers. These opinions are interspersed throughout the book.

More than any other group of educators, craft teachers should be proud that they actually practise what they teach, giving lie to George Bernard Shaw's homily: *'Those who can, do. Those who can't, teach.'*

'To teach is to learn twice'.
Joseph Joubert

TEACHING STYLE

WHAT KIND OF TEACHER ARE YOU?

Teachers come in all shapes, sizes and dispositions. Over a period we all develop a particular teaching style, just as our craft work takes on *its* own unique style.

Our teaching style is the manner in which we express ourselves and perform in the classroom. Teaching style is very much a reflection of personality, that unique entity into which we have evolved over our lives as a result of heredity and social conditioning.

How does your personality affect your teaching style? Do you 'mother' your students? Are you the vibrant, dynamic type who bounces into the classroom and never stops talking? Do you tell jokes? Or are you very calm and serene, relaxing the class with the even, mellifluous tone of your voice? Are you a bossy teacher who tries to exert her authority over the class and perceives the teaching process as being about authority and control? Or are you shy and insecure, allowing the more dominant members of the class to take over the lesson?

How does your personality affect your teaching style? Do any of these characteristics apply to you?

Bossy	Serene
Quiet	Approachable
Intimidating	Sharing
Loud	Sarcastic
Happy	Hands-on
Dithery	Relaxed
Strident	Humorous
Dynamic	Shy
Nervous	Unsure
Perfectionist	Cranky

Most of us have encountered teachers like these. The cranky or sarcastic teacher will probably have a high student drop-out rate. The shy, nervous type will tend to gain confidence with experience; the more they teach, the less insecure they will be. The bossy teacher is almost certain to have personality clashes with some students. The dithery person will need to become more organised or students may start to complain about the teacher's inefficiency.

If you are a quiet type of person, you will tend to be the same way in the classroom. If you have a loud, brash personality, this will also come across when you teach. A quiet, reserved teacher can be just as effective as the teacher who has the class in hysterics with joke-telling. Indeed, *effective teaching can encompass a whole range of personal styles.*

Whilst your personality is part of you and cannot be radically changed, it is possible to identify and modify certain negative aspects of your teaching style. Put yourself in the place of your students for a moment. How do they perceive you? Each of us has mannerisms, nervous habits, personality characteristics which, though tolerated and accepted by our families, may be irritating to our students.

Tape record your lesson or ask a friend to video-tape it. It may be a little unnerving to hear or watch yourself in action but it will assist you to identify annoying verbal and body mannerisms. It could be that the pitch of your voice is too high, or you are speaking too quickly. Perhaps your voice is too soft and you need to project more. Why not invite a fellow teacher to sit in on your lesson and observe and comment on your style. (See *Evaluating The Lesson*, page 50.)

If you are an anxious type of person, you may well communicate your nervousness to the class, who will then not perform at their best. Beat those nerves by arriving early at class, fully prepared, and take time for a pre-class cup of tea or coffee.

> *I am always nervous around new people and especially when I teach. Sometimes I don't sleep the night before a class! I have found that doing lots of preparation helps me to calm down. The day before, I pack the car with my equipment, have all my handouts photocopied and write out a short lesson plan, in case I have a mental block during class. I arrive as early as possible at the class to check for missing equipment and to try to foresee any conceivable problems. I suppose you could call me over-prepared but I feel more secure this way.*

Remember also that many of the students may be just as nervous as you are. Spend some class time on warm-up techniques (page 27) and you may find that your own anxieties dissipate.

PERSONAL PRESENTATION

A very important part of teaching style is personal presentation. In other words, you need to look the part! If you teach wearable art, then wear your creations to class. Judy Allen, fabric painting teacher of Guildford, NSW, creates a professional impression from the very start of her lessons by dressing in hand-painted clothes and accessories: bangles, ear-rings, hairclips and even painted shoes. Judy's students are immediately aware of her credentials as a fine painter, and her outfits are a source of visual inspiration for her class.

A découpeur might bring a briefcase or workbox decorated with découpage. An embroiderer could have an embroidered chatelaine and sewing box. Other teachers may choose to bring samples of their work or an album of photographs to show their students.

TEACHING ENVIRONMENT

This section discusses the best possible working conditions for the craft teacher. It is, however, unrealistic to expect that all these facilities would be available, particularly if you are teaching on a voluntary basis in a hall, club, hospital or similar venue not specifically designed for teaching. Nevertheless, there are certain steps you can take to make the teaching area more pleasant and professional.

LIGHTING

There is seldom enough natural light. If overhead fluorescent light is available, it will probably be adequate for most purposes. Should directional light be needed, you may have to provide your own, such as a small foldable lamp. Arrange the lamp so that there are no shadows across your demonstration work. A combined magnifying glass and light is useful for looking at details. Remember to take a (labelled) extension cord.

Note that lighting has an important effect on colour. Colours which you have chosen for a project may look entirely different under artificial as opposed to natural light.

HEATING AND VENTILATION

The temperature of the room should be comfortable. Hot, stuffy rooms sap the students' strength, so there should be as free a flow of air as possible. Air-conditioned comfort, especially in summer, is ideal. If the students are all restless, it may be that the room is either too hot or too cold. People tolerate conditions differently so think about changing seating positions. Cold or hot drinks may help. For lengthy courses, advise students to dress accordingly. If you are teaching at an unfamiliar venue, check first to see if there is heating or air-conditioning, then consider bringing a small fan or heater.

NOISE

Noise can be a problem for everyone if the teaching area is close to traffic. You may need to move to a back room in a building which is located on a main road. There is nothing worse than having to yell over the sound of the traffic. Carpet is a noise absorber and so are curtains and blinds.

The telephone can be distracting, so consider an answering machine in a home studio, or turn down the bell on the phone.

COLOUR

The colour of a teaching studio is important. In choosing a colour scheme, take into account the size of the studio. A small space will look larger if painted in whites or pastels. Psychologically, colour can affect your students. Warm colours tend to motivate people, while cool colours create a more peaceful, relaxed setting.

A good guide is to settle for lighter colours on walls and woodwork and place the darker colours on the floor. Chairs, curtains and blinds can be a light to medium colour. Some teachers like working on a black background and place black plastic on their tables. This is a cheap, effective, portable and wipable surface, and colour is enhanced on a black background.

FURNITURE AND FACILITIES

Furniture placement is important and should allow for repositioning. Remove any unneeded furniture at the start of the lesson — it will only get in the way. A painting class may need chairs and tables, or easels and no chairs. Fabric classes may require large cutting tables and more space to spread work. Allow time for setting up if furniture has to be rearranged to suit your lesson. Similarly, set aside a few minutes at the end for clearing away and leaving the venue tidy. This is important, especially if another class follows. It will also help you to maintain a harmonious relationship with the proprietors of the work space and your fellow teachers.

There is no 'correct' arrangement of chairs and tables for teaching. The configuration will depend on the teacher and teaching material. If you are an active teacher who likes to move around the room, you will probably prefer a U-shape. You can demonstrate in the open part of the U, and then move easily and quickly around the room inside the U. In this way, the teacher can avoid tripping over students' chairs and bags. The only problem with working from within the U-shape is that you are viewing the students' work upside down, and if you do a sample for them, they may be confused by the fact you are facing the opposite way.

Table and chair heights must be compatible and comfortable. Many otherwise well-equipped craft studios have an odd assortment of uncomfortable chairs where students are supposed to work for hours on end. Comfort in seating should be a priority. If necessary, suggest that students bring their own cushions and footstools.

If extra furniture is required, small folding card tables are useful, as are folding chairs for extra students. Note that wheelchair students will need more room.

Check the toilet facilities and ensure they are clean and that handtowels, soap, etc are available. In a home studio, if the craft is a messy one where paints, glue, etc are used, supply old towels for wiping hands, and place buckets outside the door for renewing and disposing of dirty water. This will save mess in your bathroom or kitchen. Encourage students to dispose of waste materials in a bin or bucket set aside for that purpose. Do not pour toxic materials or even dirty painting water down the sink.

Organise tea and coffee making facilities for your students. This is a courtesy gesture which is appreciated by everyone, but particularly those students who have travelled long distances, often held up in traffic. There are urns and hot drink machines available, and a small refrigerator or drink cooler can be useful in hot weather for lunches and drinks. In a home studio set up a tray or tray mobile with teabags, coffee, sugar, jug, etc and let students make their own tea and coffee. Request that students bring their own mugs — it saves on washing up. Depending on the particular circumstances, you may wish to charge a small amount to cover costs.

CLASS SIZE

The ideal class size varies from craft to craft and will depend a great deal on how much teaching space is available. Remember that crafts are practical, hands-on subjects and set an upper limit that suits you and is appropriate to the content of the lesson and the work space.

High school art and craft classes, for example, have commonly been limited to 20 students, whereas class sizes in other high school subjects may soar above thirty. In a home studio 4 to 8 students would constitute an ideal. In a shop a class of 6 to 12 people usually works well. In a large seminar room an experienced teacher could conceivably teach 15 to 20 students, but, beyond these numbers, even the best teacher will not be able to give the individual attention a practical class demands. The problem is compounded when there are several levels of ability within the one class.

At the evening college where I teach folk art, the administration has given me a class of twenty-five. How am I supposed to cope with a combination of raw beginners who need constant guidance and intermediate painters who want exciting new projects every week?

When working in a shop, evening college or similar situation, negotiate an upper class limit at the outset with the shop owner or college co-ordinator. Where there is a large enrolment above the class limit, it is preferable to run two smaller classes, graded so that beginners are together in the one class. If the class cannot be split, suggest that the extra students be placed on a waiting list. An excessively large class, particularly one of mixed ability, is neither fair to the teacher nor the students, and sometimes administrators need to be gently reminded of this.

SMOKING AND OTHER SAFETY FACTORS

Request that students do not smoke in the teaching area. Small 'No Smoking' signs can be made or purchased and placed around the room. Apart from the well documented hazards of active and passive smoking, craftspeople face additional health dangers. Firstly, there may well be flammable materials in the craft room. And secondly, crafters who smoke run the risk of ingesting toxic substances which may be on their fingers: glue, paint, glazes, sealer, varnish, etc.

For similar reasons, encourage students to wash glue and paint from their hands before eating and remind them to eat away from the work area. Likewise, clean-up should not take place at the kitchen sink if food is also prepared there.

Teachers must be aware of the toxicity of materials they use or recommend. When teaching we both have a policy of using only water-based, brush-on products in our folk and decorative painting classes. At times, adhering to this policy has been difficult because we have had to devise alternative methods of carrying out processes like antiquing for which most other teachers use toxic, oil-based products.

Avoid using spray cans in a confined area. Set up a table outdoors if you must use aerosols. Ask beforehand if there is anyone in the class with a chest condition such as asthma. A better alternative is to use brush-on products. There are brush-on equivalents for most spray products and they are usually far more cost effective than aerosols. In the case of varnishes, a brush-on finish is equal to or better than a spray finish. Expert découpeur, Nerida Singleton, of Brisbane, Qld, advocates the use of a brush in applying the 50 or so coats of varnish she uses to create the magnificent finish on her découpage hatboxes and other collectables.

Read all labels carefully. American craft products are subject to fairly rigorous testing, so check for the circular 'A.P. Non Toxic' logo which indicates the product has been certified 'non toxic' by the US Art and Crafts Materials Institute. No such standard exists for Australian made craft products, but a rule of thumb is that if the product contains solvents or is labelled 'Flammable' or 'Use in a well ventilated space', it is likely to be toxic and must be handled with care.

Dust can be a health problem in a variety of craft situations, for instance, in ceramics when preparing greenware and working with powder glazes, in woodwork, when sanding all woods, but particularly medium density fibreboard, and in any craft where metal powders are used. In all these cases, recommend the use of masks.

Découpage is a craft which requires frequent sanding. From the very first lesson Nerida Singleton emphasises the importance of wearing masks and goggles. She has a dust extractor in her studio as an additional health precaution.

Cheap disposable gloves are useful when handling dyestuffs and paints, especially oil-based products. Buy in bulk and have a supply on hand for your students. If students are reluctant to wear gloves, suggest an application of barrier cream to the hands before starting work.

It is also important to consider other safety factors such as power cords used for drills, sanders, irons, airbrushes, etc. Ensure that cords are neither frayed nor lying where people will trip over them. Have students place baskets or bags against the wall or under the table to prevent falls and to make it easier for you, as the teacher, to move around the class. Keep electrical equipment away from sinks.

You also need to think about fire safety. In a shop, studio, hall, etc, check the location of fire extinguishers and the nearest exit. Acquaint your students with this information. In a home studio, these issues are equally important. Purchase a fire extinguisher and know how to use it. Dispose of oily rags and other combustibles carefully and do not leave them in the studio where they could start a fire.

For evening classes, it is advisable to make a policy of leaving together, particularly if there are elderly people in the class.

If you are teaching regularly at a shop, hall or other venue, investigate the possibility of leaving spare equipment in a locker or cupboard, but remember to label your possessions clearly.

GENERAL CLASS SUPPLIES

There is nothing more disruptive to your lesson than to have students constantly borrowing supplies and equipment from each other. Have on hand a kit of general supplies required for your craft, the kind of items students always forget. Again, ensure that all supplies for class use are labelled with your name.

Supplies will vary from craft to craft but might include some of the following:

- Scrap paper.
- Paper towels or old rags.
- Scissors.
- Eraser.
- Pens, pencils.
- Ruler.
- Compass and set square.
- Tracing paper.
- Transfer paper.
- Glue.
- Newspaper.
- Water basins.
- Cotton buds.
- Rubber gloves.

Why not compose a checklist of general supplies for your craft and use it as a memory aid when setting up your lessons.

CHECKLIST FOR TEACHING ENVIRONMENT

- Check lighting.
- Take fan or heater.
- Re-arrange furniture, if necessary.
- Are chairs comfortable?
- Check class size.
- Take 'No Smoking' sign.
- Remember 'Safety First' regarding materials.
- Check fire safety.
- Label all your equipment.

ETHICS AND PROFESSIONALISM

THE ETHICAL TEACHER

Adopting an ethical and professional approach to teaching means acting in a manner which is considered correct for your group or craft. Many craft associations and guilds have their own 'Codes of Ethics' and it is worth familiarising yourself with these. Certain principles and values will have universal application across all craft teaching and teaching in general.

Many of these principles are based on common sense and a regard for others' rights. They include being honest, keeping confidences, not discussing the employer's business nor demeaning other teachers. Being professional involves teaching to the best of one's ability, updating skills, sharing knowledge freely and not withholding information. It also encompasses being loyal to your employer and students, maintaining a good appearance and not swearing or losing one's temper.

Students notice lapses in ethics and professionalism by the teacher:

> *I get annoyed with teachers who just sit in class and do their own thing. Perhaps working on a project for their next sale or exhibition. This seems totally unprofessional to me.*

Other examples of unprofessional behaviour are arriving late, making sarcastic comments about students' work, giving undue attention to certain students and ignoring others, teaching other teachers' designs without permission or outside the copyright specifications (see *Copyright Responsibilities*, page 13).

Sometimes, actions which are quite innocuous in one context can be unprofessional in another. It is fine to sell craft products at a home studio. But, if you also teach in a shop, it is unprofessional to sell your own products such as paints, fabrics, wood pieces and so on to the students there, unless you have permission from the proprietor to do this. If you run a home teaching studio and also teach at a shop, avoid 'poaching' students from the shop for your own studio. Indeed, you should avoid any hint that you are touting for business for your home studio when you are at the shop. If you teach at several different shops, do not discuss one proprietor's business with another. These situations can be a minefield and you need to tread very carefully.

> *We are newcomers to the craft industry, having only had our shop six months. We soon realised that some teachers we employed were less than honest. They were taking students away from our shop and teaching them at home, offering cheaper classes.*

Students, mostly from enthusiasm, pass on information about other shops, classes, products, etc in class time. This should be nipped in the bud. Suggest tactfully that it is not appropriate to discuss these matters in the shop. Similarly, if students are speaking in a derogatory manner about another teacher, let them know that you would rather not hear this. Remain firm and polite but remember that your reaction in these matters sets the standard.

All too often lapses in professionalism occur because, as a whole, craft teachers have had no formal teacher training or experience. They are so busy coping with an unfamiliar classroom situation that they take 'shortcuts' or lower their standards. An ethical, professional approach constitutes an important step towards successful teaching and should be your first priority.

CHECKLIST FOR ETHICS AND PROFESSIONALISM
- Be honest.
- No gossip.
- Hear no evil, speak no evil.
- Dress appropriately.
- Do not poach students.
- Be punctual.
- Maintain high standards of behaviour.
- Join your guild or association.

COPYRIGHT RESPONSIBILITIES

The authors feel strongly that it is the craft teacher's responsibility to have a good understanding of, and to acquaint their students with, copyright procedure. In preparing this section, the assistance of the Australian Copyright Council and the Australian Patent, Trademark and Design Office is gratefully acknowledged.

The Australian Copyright Council is a non-profit company set up to provide the arts and copyright industries with legal services, advice and publications. The Australian Patent Office is a government body where designs can be registered. See *Useful Addresses* for details.

Copyright law protects a wide range of material, including works of art and craftspeople's designs. Its aim is to reward and protect creativity and intellectual effort. Protection is free and automatic from the moment words and designs are committed to paper, craft surface or stored in any form, for example, on computer.

Copyright is usually owned by the author or creator, unless it has been sold or assigned in a contract. A small 'c' in a circle (©), followed by the name of the copyright owner with the year alongside is recommended as a general warning that the work is protected and is the creator's claim to ownership of copyright.

Note that copyright does not protect ideas, but an infringement will occur if the expression of that idea is substantially copied. For example, anyone can make a pottery bowl, but one cannot copy an artist's particular version of a pottery bowl.

A teacher should protect his or her own work, notes and designs.

> *A student who attended one of my classes was also teaching*
> *at another shop. Without my permission, she photocopied*
> *my class notes and taught them as her own work.*

Such action, without permission, constitutes an infringement. The original work has been violated. This is not fair dealing. How would you feel if your work was passed around in this way?

Janet Klepatzki of the Bavarian Folk Workshop, Camden, NSW, has a gentle warning for students and visitors in the form of a hand-painted sign saying:

> *All patterns used in workshops and classes are under*
> *copyright to Janet Klepatzki, 1992, and may not be used*
> *for teaching or profit without the Artist's permission.*

A teacher must also be certain and have proof that this work was his or her own creation. Many people seem to think that if a few words, lines or colours are altered here and there, this is permissible. Not so, as this is an infringement of copyright because a substantial part of the work is still being used. A substantial part is any part that is distinctive and recognisable to the whole work. The part need not necessarily be large.

Designs may also be formally registered, by applying to the Patent Office and paying an annual fee. The annual fee can then be paid for a period of up to sixteen years. You need to make a decision whether to register your design, which involves time and money, as opposed to using copyright, which is automatic and free.

If you would like to teach someone else's design or other material, then please seek permission from them, preferably in writing. A number of teachers, authors and designers are happy to authorise use of their work for a specific purpose and can be most generous.

It should, however, be remembered that authors, teachers and designers want to sell as many books, craft kits, pattern packets, classes, etc as possible, and they do not want their work mass-produced.

In folk and decorative painting, for instance, simply because of the acceptance of hand tracing and method-style painting, most authors and designers permit hand tracing of their designs for 'pleasure and profit'. Generally, no mechanical or electronic means of copying is allowed, except that, in some cases, it will be stated that a design can be enlarged or reduced by photocopier.

Diana Brandt, folk artist and craft writer of Leichhardt, NSW, includes a very specific and helpful notice in her book, *The Rustic Charm of Folk Art*, stating that, though the designs in her book are copyright, permission is granted to its purchaser to reproduce the designs for personal, non-commercial use or for teaching purposes only. Diana also explains her policy regarding teaching from her book:

> *Teachers are welcome to use my book as a source for teaching, but I think it is only fair that this source of inspiration be acknowledged.*

Some authors do not want their work copied in any way, except to allow brief quotations for review purposes. Teachers should always read the notice at the front of a craft book, stating if, and how, the material can be used. One teacher suggests:

> *When I want to teach a design from a craft book, I compromise by suggesting that each student purchase a copy of the book from which the design is taken. This seems the fairest solution.*

But even if each student purchases a copy of the craft book, the teacher and students will still need permission to copy the design, unless stated otherwise in the book's copyright notice.

Today, a large amount of 'copyright free' material is on the market. This covers an enormous design field. Again, it is important to read the copyright notice. You may not be allowed free reign or to publish. Sometimes only a specified number of designs may be used.

Learn more about creating your own designs. Design skills are important if you want to be a truly fine and creative teacher. Investigate courses which will help you to learn design principles and skills. The School of Colour and Design in Sydney (see Useful Addresses, page 72), for example, offers design courses for craftspeople, including workshops, two or three year certificate courses and post certificate courses for advanced students.

CHECKLIST FOR COPYRIGHT

- Read the copyright notice on books carefully.
- Write for permission to use others' designs.
- Define what you will and will not allow, regarding your own designs.
- Remind others that your work is protected with ©, your name and the year.
- Decide about registering your design.
- Acknowledge sources.
- Teach copyright ethics.
- Obtain information from the appropriate source.
- Check statements in 'copyright free' books.

ESTABLISHING FEES

Schools, TAFE, evening colleges, etc usually have set rates which they pay their teachers, and there may be little or no room for negotiation. For teachers working in shops, studios and at home, there is no system of 'award rates'. However, many craft associations and guilds have a suggested fee structure for classes and workshops with guidelines for minimum rates. These should help you in negotiating fair rates, but remember they cannot be formally enforced.

The authors recommend that, unless there are special circumstances, you do not charge below the minimum recommended rate. It is, in fact, rare that craft teachers over-charge for their services; the opposite is more often the case. This is a reflection of the general community attitude which perceives crafts as 'women's work', and craft teaching as a means by which the 'little woman' can make some 'pin money'. It is certainly time that craft teaching was recognised for what it is: a valid and skilled profession, requiring just as much expertise as any other form of teaching.

One experienced and popular craft teacher comments:

> *My fees may look high at first glance, but I have done a great deal of study in my field and have travelled overseas to learn new techniques and attend conventions. If I were teaching a business seminar, for example, people would not think twice about the tuition fees, so why this attitude to craft?*

Novice teachers should realise, however, that, unless they are a well known craftsperson in their own right, they cannot charge as much as experienced teachers. The minimum fee rate formulated by your craft association is basically intended for beginning teachers. Master teachers can and often do charge considerably more.

Sort out in your own mind exactly what your requirements are. Some craft teachers have difficulty in discussing financial matters. They equivocate about what they want and often undervalue their own talent:

> *As a craft teacher, I hate having to discuss money and fees. I always feel uncomfortable when these matters are raised. When a shop owner asks me my rates, I usually say: 'Pay me whatever you think is fair' or 'Pay me what you pay your other teachers', without even asking what that rate is.*

Write a list of expenses: travel, time and preparation. It is amazing how many hidden costs there are.

When dealing with shops, settle financial matters at the outset. If your craft association has printed fee guidelines, take them with you. Be specific about your criteria. Do you want a flat fee for the day or half day? Or do you want to be paid per student? In this case, specify a minimum number of students which will make the class financially viable for you. Discuss the number of hours you will teach and the maximum number of students you will accept. Will there be a cancellation fee paid to you if the shop owner has to cancel the class at the last moment? Once you have negotiated these matters, confirm everything in writing, by fax or letter, and keep a copy.

You must then decide what action you will take if, for example, you turn up to class one day and there are only two students, but the specified minimum was six. Most ethical shop proprietors will pay you the full agreed amount and will often have covered themselves for just this kind of eventuality.

For a one-off workshop, the proprietor may have only taken deposits. You could perhaps negotiate what you both consider to be a fair fee. Ideally, however, this possibility should have been discussed at the time of organising the workshop. And in any case, the shop owner should have been aware of the small size of the class several days earlier and contacted you to discuss the situation, with one possible scenario being cancellation of the class.

See also *Running Classes at Home*, page 54, *Teaching Through Shops and Studios*, page 61 and *Business Practicalities*, page 70.

CHECKLIST FOR FEES
- Contact association or guild about fee guidelines.
- Ask other teachers.
- Settle fees at the outset.
- Negotiate details: flat fee or paid per student, minimum and maximum numbers, etc.
- Keep records.

JOINING A PROFESSIONAL ASSOCIATION

As discussed earlier, there are associations and guilds for most crafts. The Crafts Councils throughout Australia have information about the major groups. See page 72. You will find membership of your association to be an invaluable resource. Meetings and newsletters will help you to share ideas with fellow crafters, update skills and keep in touch with the latest trends and products.

Most associations have a teachers' register on which your name, address, phone number and teaching interests can be listed. If enquiries about classes in a certain area are received, the association can supply names of appropriate teachers. Some associations even offer teacher certification or accreditation programmes. Most often, however, these are assessed on the teacher's craft ability and not their ability to teach.

Note that fees paid to your professional association are tax deductible but receipts must be kept. See also pages 70-1.

CONTINUING EDUCATION

An important aspect of professionalism is extending and updating craft skills at courses, seminars and workshops. Teachers need to keep abreast of the new products and techniques being developed constantly in today's expanding craft world.

In addition, attending classes is your chance to be a *student* again. But remember that you also bring with you the added ability of assessing the lesson as a *teacher*. You can learn much from this experience.

> There is nothing I enjoy more than being a student in somebody else's class. People ask me why I attend so many classes. It's because I am always wanting to learn more. So many new ideas are emerging and I want to be part of them. Besides, teachers tend to forget what it is like to be a student; the anxieties, the frustrations and the sense of achievement when you get it right!

Just as association dues are tax deductible, the teachers can also claim part of their self-education expenses. See page 71. Note, however, that the cost of classes undertaken prior to beginning to earn money as a teacher is not tax deductible.

ESTABLISHING REALISTIC AIMS
AND OBJECTIVES

IDENTIFYING TEACHING SKILLS

Plan lessons so that students will succeed at the required tasks. If students cannot master the skill by the end of the lesson/course, the fault may not be with them, but with the teacher.

Many students go away from a class disheartened, saying: 'I can't sew/paint/pot/embroider/do this or that!' It would be easy to condemn these students for lack of ability, but it is more often the case that such comments are a reflection of poor preparation by the teacher who has not formulated and taught appropriate aims and objectives.

It is vital to examine a project or teaching material and break it down into its component skills. Write down, in list form, the practical skills you aim to have the students master by the end of the course. This list becomes the 'aims and objectives' for the course.

You could even hand out this list to the students so that they can see the direction in which the course is heading. In this way, too, you can deter them from demanding to learn techniques or projects beyond their current ability level.

How do you decide which skills to teach? They need to be:

- Appropriate to the level of the students' ability.
- Useful. There is no point in teaching a skill which your students may rarely, if ever, use.

In a beginners' embroidery course, for example, the teacher would introduce some basic stitches. The final objective of the course might be to create an embroidered garden. But the first step is to isolate the skills requires to stitch the flowers. Each type of stitch would be a separate skill, and five skills might be chosen: back-stitch, running stitch, straight-stitch, lazy daisy and French knot. The easiest stitches are taught first. Once the students have been taught a couple of stitches and have practised these individually, several skills could be combined, for instance, a circlet of lazy daisy stitches with a French knot in the middle to make a daisy.

Don't spend too long practising isolated skills out of context — it leads to boredom. Just as the piano student wants to play a piece rather than constantly practise scales, the craft student is just dying to make something. Don't let that enthusiasm wane. As soon as individual skills have been practised and mastered, you should combine them in a way that creates something tangible, even if it is as simple as an embroidered daisy.

Breaking a lesson up into its component parts will help you to teach in an organised and efficient way.

Once goals are set, you must then consider how you will present, practise and revise these skills. See *Teaching Strategies and Techniques*, page 34.

SAMPLE LESSON PLANS

Writing out a lesson plan is one way of sorting out your aims and objectives and is a very useful exercise.

Here are some sample lesson plans covering a variety of crafts and situations, including one-off workshops and continuous series of lessons. We have chosen the popular crafts of folk art and patchwork, but the principles are universal and can be applied to any craft. The lesson plans were prepared by expert teachers of each craft and serve as examples which you can analyse and adapt. Each is formatted in the particular teacher's own way. There is no one correct way of setting out a lesson plan — choose a format which works for you.

INTRODUCTORY PATCHWORK

COURSE DURATION
Seven weeks. 2 hour class each week.

AIMS AND OBJECTIVES
- To acquaint students with different types of patchwork: American, English, hand appliqué, curved piecing, quick method cutting and an introduction to machine quilting.
- To work with colour and use of pattern and texture.

TEACHING STRATEGIES
Lesson One
- The teacher provides ideas and samples on how to use the first block (a unit of patchwork design, usually square, used alone or repeated to quilt an overall pattern in a quilt top.)

- The students draw a simple nine patch block or pattern.
- They colour in the block and choose their fabric for the project.
- All the equipment, uses and options are explained. Note: Not all equipment is needed for the first few lessons.
- Students should go home stimulated about patchwork. Their homework is to wash their chosen fabrics.

Lesson Two

- Making templates (a pattern made from plastic, which can be cut with scissors).
- Cutting fabric.
- Techniques of hand sewing.

Lessons 3 to 7 continue along similar lines. The teacher supplies notes on all aspects of the lessons.

BASIC MATERIALS REQUIRED

- HB and H pencil.
- White pencil.
- Eraser.
- Blue fabric marking pen.
- Permanent marking pen.
- Paper scissors.
- Fabric scissors.
- Embroidery crewel needles, size 8 or 9.
- Lace pins.
- Thimble — metal or leather.
- Thread for hand sewing — cotton or polycotton.
- Thread for quilting.
- Bees' wax.
- Plastic sheets for templates.
- Quilting hoop.

- Polyester wadding.
- Tailor's awl.
- Plastic pockets.
- Note book.
- Clear plastic ruler approximately 38 cm (15") plus.
- Large sheet graph paper.

FOLK ART WORKSHOP

PROJECT
Australian Wildflowers on a Tray.

LEVEL
Intermediate.

PREREQUISITES
Mastery of surface preparation and of basic round brush strokes, and some experience with a flat brush required.

TIME REQUIRED
Six hours.

AIMS AND OBJECTIVES
To acquaint students with painting three wildflowers: the waratah, flannel flower and wattle in folk art style.

SKILLS TO BE TAUGHT
- Floated colour with a flat brush to create shadows and highlights.
- Liner work accents.
- Finishing techniques: crackling and antiquing.

MATERIALS REQUIRED

- Wood piece: wooden tray, 40 cm (16″) long, 30 cm (12″) wide.
- Artists' acrylic paints: medium red, white, yellow, ochre, medium yellow green, dark blue-green, dark brown, medium grey, black.
- Brushes: sponge brush, 2 cm (1″) base-coating brush, No. 3 round brush, No. 10 flat brush, liner brush.
- Miscellaneous: sandpaper, water jar, palette, cotton buds, sample board, crackle medium, water-based satin varnish.

PRE-CLASS PREPARATION BY STUDENTS

Sand and base-coat tray in dark green. Transfer pattern with white transfer paper.

TEACHING PLAN

Morning

- Base in waratahs on tray. Practise floated colour on paper, then float shadows and highlights on waratahs.
- Practise flannel flower strokes on paper, then paint flannel flower petals and centres on tray.

Afternoon

- Float shading on flannel flowers.
- Paint leaves and stems of waratah and flannel flowers.
- Add liner work accents: stamens, veins, etc.
- Paint wattle dots as filler flowers to balance the composition.
- Crackle flowers and apply acrylic antiquing to cracks.
- Varnish if time allows.

TEACHING STRATEGIES

- Easel demonstration of each new technique. Teacher paints design (twice actual size) with class on sample board.
- Teacher paints sample for each student of each technique.

TEACHING AIDS

- Sample finished tray.
- Easel and sample boards.
- Whiteboard for diagrams.
- Step-by-step painted charts of each flower.
- Photograph of finished project for each student.
- Full instructions printed on handouts.

CHOOSING A PROJECT

When choosing a project for a workshop or class, there are a number of factors which should be considered.

LEVEL OF DIFFICULTY
Is it appropriate to the level of ability of your students? Is it challenging? Will they succeed?

WHAT SKILLS DOES THE PROJECT TEACH?
Will it introduce a good range of new techniques?

IS IT ARTISTICALLY APPEALING?
Visual impact, subject matter, colours, design composition.

TIME REQUIRED

Most teachers seriously underestimate the time required to complete a project. Ideally students (particularly beginners) should leave the class/course with the piece well on the way to completion. Similarly, if it is a large project with the design repeated elsewhere, the repetitive sections can be done at home as long as the basic design components and techniques have been mastered in class.

When running a workshop over several consecutive days, think carefully before giving homework each night — students are tired after a long day and should not have to go home and do hours of work.

Estimate the time it took you to craft the piece, then multiply by 2 if you work at average speed, by 3 or 4 if you are a fast worker. This will give an idea of how many hours/days to allow for students to finish the piece in class.

COST

For beginners, try to keep the cost of materials down. Smaller pieces are usually better for beginners anyway — they tend to be intimidated and overwhelmed by large projects.

In a quilting class, start with a small item made from one or more quilt panels such as a cushion or a small wall hanging, rather than a full size quilt. In a folk art class, major works (floorcloths, large pieces of furniture, etc) should generally be the preserve of the advanced painter. Begin with wooden cut-outs, a plaque, a doorstop, a key-ring, and so on. For a découpage class, begin with a small box or plaque rather than a hat box or screen. In leadlighting, start with a lightcatcher rather than a large panel or a three dimensional article like a box. And so on.

When planning a beginners' kit, consider the cost factor and keep materials to a minimum. Beginners do not need a whole range of fancy equipment!

SPECIAL NEEDS

If you are teaching students with special needs such as sight problems or arthritis, choose suitable projects. See page 48.

LISTING CLASS REQUIREMENTS

A well-organised teacher will present students with a comprehensive list of class requirements well ahead of the class itself. How this list is presented will depend on the circumstances. For a block of lessons, you could simply jot a note on the board at the end of each class to explain what special materials are needed for the next lesson. However, at the start of block lessons, or for a one-off workshop, you will need to prepare a formal written requirements list. Usually this is supplied to the administrator or shop owner who will then distribute the information to students. If you teach at home, sheets could be mailed to or collected by students.

Often in a shop or evening college situation, this requirements list is the teacher's first contact with the students. It creates the initial impression, and, as we all know, first impressions count a great deal. Make your pre-class information look professional. Consider a logo at the top of the sheet. Calligraphers could hand-letter their lists. Otherwise, write clearly or preferably type the sheet.

If you have a computer and printer, use it to prepare the requirements lists, and they can be quickly and easily amended for future use.

The material included in the requirements list is very much dependent on the particular craft, but, in general, it should state:

- The title of the class or workshop.
- Teacher's name.
- Venue.
- Date and times.
- Cost.
- Level of difficulty.
- Materials needed, if any. If you are providing some or
  all the materials yourself, make sure students know this.

Teachers may also need to include instructions on how to prepare a project if this is required. In some crafts, like folk art, wood may have to be base-coated and patterns transferred before class, so this information needs to be given out with the requirements list.

In preparing patterns, consider copying them onto tracing rather than cartridge paper. A tracing paper pattern makes design transfer much easier.

Students also appreciate information about lunch arrangements. Should they bring their own? Is there a cafe or snack bar close by? A small map showing the venue and parking could also be included.

See page 65 for a sample pre-class information sheet.

CREATING A POSITIVE CLASSROOM ATMOSPHERE

Agood start is one of the most significant factors in making the lesson a success. Be calm and relaxed, create a mood for success, for students to work and learn in a free and positive way.

SETTING THE MOOD: ICE BREAKING AND WARM-UP TECHNIQUES

From the outset, be quite direct. Maintain good eye contact and smile: 'Today, we are going to make a pot, paint a doll, learn to spin, piece our patchwork, etc!' Try creative visualisation, quietly present a vision of the completed article. See pages 41-3.

We have all seen the TV presenter walking on stage to a cheering audience. This may not be entirely due to his popularity. The audience has, of course, been warmed up beforehand, usually with music or a comedian. The crowd is in a good mood, laughing on cue.

Like the live TV audience, your class needs to be 'warmed up'. This doesn't mean you have to sing or tell jokes. You don't even need to do formal warm-up activities. Keep it relaxed and casual.

Start by telling students about yourself: how and when you started crafting, how long you have been teaching, and so on. Try giving a brief history of the craft. In a doll-making class, for example, you could mention that the earliest known doll was found in an Egyptian tomb, dated about 2000 BC. In a patchwork class, you might tell students that patchwork was used as therapy for soldiers recuperating from the Crimean War. Such snippets of history are not only interesting but act as useful warm-up techniques.

Ask the class questions. Use their names (see below): 'Mary, why did you come today? Sally, how did you hear about these classes? John, did you have far to come?' Ask questions as you move around the room, handing out kits. At this stage it is not advisable to put the questions to every student as it would take too much time. Here is one effective technique:

> *As a warm-up for my classes, I give a little prize for the person who has come farthest to class. This involves the students in a lively but cheerful debate as to who travelled the longest distance.*

Another teacher comments:

I find music has a soothing effect on students, if it is played quietly in the background.

Denise Ferris of Studio One, Findon, SA, has some wonderful ideas for making her students feel 'at home'. She likes to set the scene by making paper placemats for each student. They are simply A3 size photocopies with an extra pattern or with some verses or sayings related to the project. For a ceramic cat, the placemat might have sayings such as:

The purr of a cat is like the sigh of an angel.

A home without a cat is just a house.

When Denise teaches teddy bear projects, she serves teddy bear biscuits with morning tea. Denise also gives class members a small ceramic teddy bear as a bonus. They can practise a new technique on this before working on their actual project. Fast students can paint the ceramic teddy while waiting for others to catch up. And a little gift on the table when students arrive makes them feel special.

If the subject is roses, Denise will have a beautiful vase of roses on the table to inspire her class. A lesson on strawberries will be reinforced by real strawberries, ready to be used as models and then later consumed. Similarly, when Deborah teaches her students to paint florals, she brings a small bouquet of flowers from her cottage garden for each student.

The teacher's purpose is to set the class thinking. To guide them gently into the world of art and craft, to help them forget for a few hours the stresses of the outside world.

Students come to craft classes for many and varied reasons. They may have failed at the last class. Perhaps they have been advised by their doctor to take up a hobby. Maybe they have just retired, or they came only because their friend has talked them into it. For young mothers, it may be a chance to get away from the kids for a few hours and pursue an interest of their own. The teacher's job is to meld this disparate group into a class of creative and positive learners.

Set the right mood from the beginning. Be prepared, be early, set your work out. Look friendly and efficient.

Put yourself in the place of the student for a moment. This may be their first lesson and they are feeling a little apprehensive. Some students may have travelled long distances. Have the kettle boiled. Count heads, laugh and smile, make them feel welcome. Indicate the toilet facilities, explain lunch arrangements and other practicalities.

NAMES

Before the class, phone the shop and obtain a list of names. Memorise them. In class introduce yourself first, obtain the students' names and write them down in order of seating. Refer to this throughout the lesson. Call the students by name from the list. They are always genuinely surprised and pleased to think that you know their name. Alternatively, have name cards prepared for them. This helps students to get to know one another. Inexpensive self adhesive stickers (available from newsagents) are excellent for this, or purchase plastic tags with a pin and removable name card and use them over and over again. For something different, there are badge-making tools available or wooden blanks which could be painted or neatly printed.

I like to make the students in my class feel special by creating a calligraphy name sticker for each of them. I am not an expert calligrapher — I use a felt tip calligraphy pen from the newsagent and refer to a lettering book as a guide.

NERVOUS?

Your own nervousness can be overcome with practice. Write small cue cards or prompters. Stand in front of a long mirror, rehearse the lesson out loud, repeat this performance. With experience, and especially once you begin to speak about and demonstrate a skill you know well, the 'butterflies' will soon disappear.

LATE ARRIVALS

We have all had students who arrive late, very apologetic. They continue to be apologetic and regale us with long stories, albeit important to them, but taking up valuable class time. In turn, it reminds another student to relate further events including how the dog ate their fabric. All this is very time-consuming, and you must take charge and take time to smooth things over. Only you can decide how long to wait for latecomers. (See page 45.)

SETTLING THE CLASS

Should the lesson start badly, it is often difficult to repair the situation. Remember that a chaotic beginning can mean the failure of the whole lesson.

When you are ready to start the actual teaching process, draw the class to attention. Some teachers use their voice somewhat louder. Others just stand quietly, waiting for silence. A system which can work with a large class is simply to raise one's hand. Tell the class beforehand what this signal means. Then when your hand goes up, one student tells another and the message is soon spread.

PREPARATION OF TEACHING AIDS

BLACKBOARDS AND WHITEBOARDS

In preparing and conducting a lesson, there are many teaching aids available. The most basic would be a blackboard or whiteboard. Although these *should* be basic equipment in every craft classroom, this is often not the case. Consider purchasing your own portable board. Corkboard/whiteboard combinations are available from chain stores. Butcher's paper can be attached to the corkboard, using drawing pins or bulldog clips. Such boards are good for student participation and ideas, as well as diagrams, summaries and prompt notes. Whiteboards tend to be better than blackboards because there is no chalk dust, a problem in a craft like china painting where the area must be dust-free.

To create your own whiteboard, purchase a sheet of white laminated board from a timber supplier or kitchen cabinet maker. This makes a wipable surface suitable for spirit pens. A sheet of craftwood, padded then covered with calico, is excellent for pinning fabric samples, etc.

STEP-BY-STEP GUIDES

Step-by-step guides are also valuable. Photographs, placed in plastic sleeves, can be numbered and passed around the class. In painting classes, step-by-step sample boards are very useful to students. Some folk art teachers give each student a small painted sample of the flower or leaf, showing the individual strokes and the finished motif. If the teacher actually paints the sample in front of each student, the exercise becomes even more valuable. In needlecraft, it is helpful to have samples of the garment, quilt, etc at various stages of completion. In china painting, a teacher could present step-by-step samples of the piece showing the effects of each firing.

SLIDES

Slides can be a good way of getting the message across, but there must be heavy curtains or blinds to darken the room. Although a screen is useful, you can always project the slides onto a plain, bare wall or a whiteboard. Note, however, that long slide sessions can be boring and students tend to nod off in the dark. Keep the slide display short and to the point, and ensure each slide is correctly focussed. Store slides, labelled and numbered, in a plastic slide tray or carousel, ready to be used.

Slide projectors are notoriously unreliable, so do not count on your slides. Always have an alternative prepared.

OVERHEAD PROJECTORS

Overhead projectors are a fine teaching tool. They allow you to face the class whilst drawing diagrams or writing notes. Areas of the overhead display can be easily masked off by covering with a piece of paper.

Overhead projectors are light and portable, and there are now models which fold up to briefcase size. Overhead transparencies can be made on a black and white or colour photocopier by feeding in acetate transparency sheets rather than paper. Diagrams and text can be enlarged or reduced, as appropriate.

Do not crowd too much information onto each transparency. A simple diagram or a few carefully chosen points are better.

Remember to have spare projector bulbs with you. There is nothing worse than basing a presentation on OHP transparencies and then having the bulb blow and your transparencies rendered useless.

VIDEOS

Videos are well established as teaching aids, provided that the ancillary equipment is available. Note that they should be used as a supplement to your teaching, rather than taking up the whole lesson. Do not hesitate to stop the video and replay important parts.

The video could be passed from student to student and viewed at home. Have several copies to rent out. Libraries also have videos for borrowing, and will often obtain special videos for you.

There is now a wide range of craft videos available, including the 'View 'n Do' series from Plaid Enterprises (available through DMC in Australia). Beware mail ordering videotapes direct from the US for use in Australia — the operating systems are different, and the video will need to be converted, at considerable cost.

HANDOUTS

Information sheets, notes and handouts can be very useful to students, particularly as a future reference or if they have to complete the project at home. Provide adequate instructional notes for your students so that they can get on with doing their craft rather than feverishly writing down instructions. It is almost impossible to listen, work *and* write notes at the same time. Being creative involves certain areas of the brain which are not necessarily compatible with those required for taking down notes.

Preparing and duplicating sheets can involve considerable work on your part. Where possible, have the shop or institution photocopy the sheets. If they are reluctant to do this, students could be charged a small fee for the notes, or the cost could be built into the class fee.

Consider presenting sheets, particularly to a beginners' class, in clear plastic sleeves. These can be purchased cheaply in bulk from chain stores. Suzanne Kelly, calligrapher of Beecroft, NSW, presents her beginning students with an impressive kit containing notes on the history of lettering styles, a basic alphabet to use as a model, a slope card and some sample calligraphy papers. Such a kit creates an instant impression of professionalism and efficiency.

It is important to retain your notes and patterns for future use. Store the originals in plastic sleeves and file carefully.

If you have access to a computer and printer, you can create impressive class notes and not have to store reams of paper in folders. Notes stored as computer files can be easily amended and personalised. In order to add dates and times or the name of an institution or shop, make a copy of the file and edit it accordingly. The computer can create attractive heading templates to use over and over again. If you have access to a scanner, personal diagrams and illustrations can be cut and pasted electronically into your notes. Alternatively, experiment with the graphics system on the computer to make diagrams.

EASELS

There are numerous types of easel available from art shops, all portable, and some table top versions. Some easels have a board attached upon which to rest your work. The cheaper easels often require a firm board to hold your work steady. Portable blackboards and whiteboards can also be propped on the easel.

COLOUR PHOTOCOPYING

Colour photocopying remains expensive, but it is a wonderful time-saver and an excellent teaching aid. Actual sample boards or enlarged photographs of the project can be photocopied.

COLOUR PHOTOGRAPHS

Colour photographs are a cheaper alternative to colour photocopying. If you order a large number of duplicate prints at once, you can often negotiate a good price. Shop around. Your local photo developing shop may offer a discount, even for an order of several dozen copies. Photo developing laboratories and commercial photographers offer excellent prices on multiple duplication of the one print. Orders of over 100 prints can work out as low as 30 or 40 cents each.

A PERSONAL ASSISTANT

Another valuable teaching aid, particularly for larger classes, is a personal assistant, just as artisans sometimes have apprentices. Often you have a promising student, one whom you feel would make a good teacher. Why not ask if they would be prepared to assist you and have on the spot training?

CHECKLIST OF TEACHING AIDS
- Finished project.
- Blackboard/whiteboard.
- An easel.
- Sample boards.
- Step-by-step charts or samples.
- Diagrams.
- Photographs and colour photocopies.
- Slides.
- Overhead projector transparencies.
- Videos.
- Instructional notes.
- Samples of materials to be used: fabric, paper, colour swatches etc.

TEACHING STRATEGIES
AND TECHNIQUES

As discussed in 'Creating a Positive Classroom Atmosphere', be early to class, settle the students and complete the introductions. During the lesson, remember the following general points:

- Good manners.
- Good eye contact — involve the whole class.
- Be positive.
- Ask questions.
- Smile.
- Check your body language — you are in charge.

When you teach, you should appear approachable, open to questions. Greet each question with a smile and encourage comment. Put yourself in the place of your students and recall how you felt as a newcomer to your craft field.

PRESENTATION TECHNIQUES

It is difficult for students to simultaneously work on their craft piece and grasp everything you are saying. When you want to make an important point, ask students to stop work and listen. Get their attention by saying something like: 'Stop work for a moment please and look up here!'

In presenting new material, aim to maintain the attention of the whole class, not just one or two while the others sit twiddling their thumbs. This is why it is counter-productive, except in very small classes, to introduce new material by going around to each student and showing them individually. Individual demonstrations have their place, but as a reinforcement technique after the main presentation.

Begin with a whole class demonstration, such as an easel presentation. With a small class, ask them to come and sit or stand around you as you demonstrate, but be sure that they can all see. Demonstrate again, perhaps using a different approach.

Ask the students to tell you what you did. Ask them if they understood. Identify any source of confusion or lack of understanding at this stage and remedy it now. More experienced teachers will be able to anticipate their students' areas of weakness before this stage and point these out in the demonstrations.

Make sure that you repeat instructions at least one more time than you think is necessary! Repetition and, hence, patience are vital.

Have the students do a practice sample of the task. Reinforce what you have just taught by having them do it again, and again!

When deciding how to present your material, remember that people learn in different ways. Some people are visual learners — they learn primarily through seeing the work presented. Others are social learners — they like to interact with you and the other students and this is how they learn best. Yet others are analytical and respond to a chart, diagram or orderly list written up on the board.

Try to present new material using a variety of these approaches. Show them the technique, talk about it, write up the salient points on the board, ask some key questions.

If it is a difficult concept, try to relate it back to something familiar to the students. Use an example or analogy from everyday life. Deborah, in her decorative painting classes, uses lots of cooking and food analogies:

> *I compare mixing black paint into another colour as adding food colouring to icing — just a little at a time, or disaster! Paint consistency is compared to food consistency: like pouring cream, thin gravy, icing, etc. Students seem to relate well to these examples.*

Always revise the material you have taught previously, not just at the beginning of each lesson but throughout the lesson. Explain again, or better still, ask class members to recap.

DEALING WITH INDIVIDUAL STUDENTS

Once you have demonstrated to the whole class, it is time to move around the room, do a sample for each student or deal with individual questions. It is vital to circulate and check on what students are doing *before* they get into trouble.

A minute or two spent with each student on a regular basis throughout the lesson is better than spending 15 minutes with them and then not returning for the rest of the lesson.

Make sure that your time is not monopolised by the more demanding students. Students should feel that they have all been fairly treated. This does not mean that the teacher has to spend exactly the same amount of time with each student, but remember that imagined or actual unequal treatment is a sure way of losing students. See also *Criticising Students' Work,* page 40.

Spend some time towards the end of the lesson with each student, assessing their work. Discuss the technique, colours, design, etc and, if appropriate, make suggestions for finishing the project.

QUESTIONING TECHNIQUES

Don't simply 'talk at' the class. Involve your students in the learning process. Make them think! Keep them alert and focussed on the task at hand.

Throw questions over to the class. Ask them what the next step might be, why are you using this particular colour or fabric, would another do equally well, which piece of equipment is appropriate for this task, could another technique be substituted, and so on.

If they are forced to work out an answer for themselves, students will learn and remember better.

PACING THE LESSON

The pace of a lesson is vital to its success. When planning a lesson, bear in mind that people learn more in the morning and that energy levels are lower after lunch.

Unfortunately, the way a lesson turns out will often be very different to this. After lunch a teacher may realise he or she is running out of time. The teacher rushes the students through their work at a time when they are least inclined to learn efficiently. If possible, plan the heavy workload and difficult tasks for the morning.

The pace of the lesson will not be right for every student in the class. Try to aim at the crafter of average ability. If the better students have time to spare, give them extension activities such as variations of what has been taught. Have them work on the repeat motif or the border on their project.

Weaker students will always be a little behind. But you cannot hold up the lesson indefinitely while waiting for them to catch up. Reassure these students and check that they have worked satisfactory examples of each new technique before the class is over.

Pacing also involves timing yourself. Use a lesson plan to divide the lesson into its basic components, then estimate realistically how long it will take to teach each element. Allow time for warm-up and settling the class in your estimate. Do you spend too long on the easy parts of the project or too much time in idle conversation and then not have time to cover every point? Keep an eye on the time — don't let those valuable minutes tick away in vain.

Try making a note on your lesson plan as to where you should be in the lesson at a particular time. Think of organising a dinner party. You make up a timetable: oven on at 7 pm, put the meat in the oven at 7.15, heat the soup at 7.30, serve soup at 8 pm, serve meat at 9 pm, etc.

Using the Fantasy Marble Case Study in the 'Teaching Through Shops and Studios', page 64, here is a schedule for teaching a marble faux finish on a wooden stool to a beginners' workshop:

- *10 am to 10.15:* Welcome, introductions, distribute kits, name tags, settle class.
- *10.15 to 10.30 am:* Brief outline of teacher's experience with faux finishes. Short historical background. Outline what workshop will achieve. Open kit, discuss contents.
- *10.30 to 12 pm:* Sand stool and sample board. Base-coat board. Demonstrate and teach liner brushwork. Practise gold liner work detailing for stool on paper. Base-coat stool. Select colours.
- *12 pm to 12.30 pm:* Teach sponging techniques on sample board.
- *12.30 to 1 pm:* Lunch.
- *1 pm to 3 pm:* Sponge stool. Marble effects on sample board. Marble stool. Liner work on stool. Drying, sanding, varnishing.
- *3 pm to 3.30 pm:* Wind down, discussion, exhibit, feedback, clean up, close lesson.

An important part of pacing the lesson is to allow sufficient time to close the class in a relaxed and positive way. If you want to tell students what is happening in the following lesson, the discussion needs to take place before the end of the lesson. If people are packing up, talking, saying farewells, rushing off to pick up the kids, they are not in the frame of mind to comprehend instructions clearly. Remember to thank students for coming and ask if they enjoyed the class.

ENCOURAGING CREATIVITY AND ORIGINALITY

What sets truly excellent teachers apart from their peers is the ability to engender creative and original work in their students. Such teachers will encourage students to find their own unique way rather than slavishly follow the teacher's example. Pamela Jones, a versatile artist and proprietor of The Folk Art Studio in Fairlight, NSW says:

> *I have a structured programme of teaching which emphasises learning all the basics in a steady progression. This approach eventually enables students to make informed judgments on which way they want to direct their talents. Because of my formal art training, I have been able to help students and other teachers to expand their own potential without having to refer to books all the time.*

Many teachers, however, work from commercial patterns and books. They do not create their own designs and, therefore, find it hard to encourage their students to be original and creative. In many situations, this may be quite satisfactory. In the increasingly popular craft of decorative painting, for example, tracing and method painting are accepted practices. Students, in the initial stages, do not need to be able to draw. But even within the limits of tracing a pattern, students are acquainting themselves with the form and flow of the design. Each painted piece they do serves to build up their confidence, so that one day they may try a new idea and experiment for themselves.

Teachers who would like to improve their design skills could undertake a course in design such as those described on page 15. Such knowledge places the teacher in a better position to encourage those same skills in others.

As Pamela Jones says above, teachers need to teach and consolidate basic skills, but once these are mastered, even your beginners can be encouraged to follow their own interests and create something original. In a beginners' needlecraft course, it might be as simple as helping your students choose their own fabric colours, rather than exactly copying your choices. Some students will always want to reproduce exactly what you have done, and that is fine if it makes them happy. Remember that students will have different expectations of what they want to achieve in class, and a carbon copy of your work may well be their ultimate goal.

But many others are just waiting for some guidance as to how they can adapt and extend what they have learnt. Whatever approach you adopt, it is important to encourage your students to at least appreciate good design principles and have an open mind to new techniques and ideas.

STUDENTS' EXPECTATIONS

You and your students may well have different expectations of what is to be achieved in the course. And this can be a source of conflict, unless it is sorted out early. It is important to discuss aims and objectives at the outset. Be specific. Outline the skills they will learn. Show them the kind of projects they will do. You may even want to give them a list of your aims. (See page 19.)

Students, naturally enough, want to achieve something tangible each lesson. In their minds, this could take the form of a new project every time, something they can show off to family and friends. How can this attitude be reconciled with your own concerns as a teacher to spend time reinforcing and consolidating craft skills?

Remind students that each new skill they acquire is a tangible achievement in itself. Emphasise the importance of a good grounding in theory and technique.

Reach a compromise between keeping the students happy (and remember that often they are paying substantial amounts to do your class), and giving them a good foundation in that particular craft.

It is also important to recognise that craft is about making things, so don't spend too long working practice examples. In a beginners' course, if the class makes only one project in the semester, they could well feel they haven't achieved much and may not return next semester. But, by contrast, if you teach ten pieces in ten weeks, unless those projects are small and very carefully chosen, students may not have learnt much about craft techniques.

It is up to you as teacher to resolve these issues with your students in a way which works for both parties.

GAUGING THE CLASSROOM CLIMATE

There are warning signs that the lesson is not proceeding as it should. Be alert to these and take quick action to retrieve the situation.

Observe the class carefully. The following are usually signs that the students have not comprehended your instructions.

- Heavy sighs and frowns.
- Students asking other students what to do.
- Blank looks and eyes 'glazing over'.
- Comments under the breath.
- Students asking too many questions.
- Students all asking the same kind of question.

You must take immediate action. Identify the source of their confusion. Ask if they all understood that procedure. Ask for a show of hands.

Demonstrate again. Try a different approach. Remember that people learn in different ways. Show them the technique, talk about it, write a summary on the board. Ask the students to explain to you what you have just done. Then have them do it and check the results yourself.

Observe the behaviour of the students themselves. Perhaps some students are talking too much and not listening. One student may be taking over. Sometimes there may be an unnerving silence, indicating tension.

Should a negative atmosphere develop, you can act in a variety of ways. Take a tea break. Or chat about everyday matters in an attempt to relax everyone. Humour is good here. You could relate an amusing anecdote. Or do some revision. Try questions and answers, with a little prize for correct replies.

If students appear disheartened, a statement by you to the effect that you *never* have failures, although the first attempts may have been rather pathetic, is often received with surprise, then laughter. Sometimes they forget that the teacher had to learn. One does not wake up in the morning and overnight become an expert at calligraphy, painting or, indeed, any craft. See 'Motivating Your Students', page 41.

CRITICISING STUDENTS' WORK

You can and should criticise a student's work where needed, but this must be done tactfully and constructively without undermining the student's self confidence. Always try to find something good to say about a student's work first, then phrase the criticism as a suggestion or question. Ask the student what *they* think about their work.

Often students are obviously unhappy with what they have done but lack the knowledge and experience to identify and correct the problem. One student comments:

> *I was unhappy with the way my embroidery looked, and told the teacher I had a problem. But when she came over she said, 'That looks good', and passed on to the next student. It was as if she was too apathetic to bother helping me fix the problem.*

A good teacher does not dismiss a student's request for help. Instead, the teacher will use his or her resources to help the student correct the problem. Firstly, the teacher might ask the student if they can identify what's wrong. The teacher can then offer some clues: Is it the colour? Is it too large? Too small? Is the shape wrong? Does it need more definition? Is it too cluttered? And so on.

Once you have both identified the problem, discuss how it can be fixed. As teacher, you can provide some 'leads', but try to let the student come up with a solution of their own.

Take time to evaluate students' work at the end of the lesson:

> *I always allow time towards the end of the lesson to see their work. I sit down and they come up one at a time. Students enjoy this individual attention and the opportunity to discuss work.*

MOTIVATING STUDENTS

The 'self fulfilling prophecy' approach to teaching states that if you and your students believe they will succeed, there is a high probability that they will indeed be successful. By the same reasoning, if they expect or are expected to fail, chances are they will indeed fail. Student success is all about expectations: your expectations of them and their expectations of themselves.

It is the teacher's task to inspire students to believe that they will be able to master the tasks set for them. Your students need to have confidence in you, and you in them. One teacher says:

I always tell my students: 'If I can do it, you can do it!'

As teacher, you need to be a motivator, the eternal optimist. You must believe that you can teach anyone to be competent in your craft, if they have the inclination and dedication.

CREATING SUCCESSFUL SITUATIONS

Remember our earlier discussion about setting appropriate aims and objectives. The teacher should aim to create learning tasks in which students achieve success. The tasks you set should be challenging but within the student's reach.

In reality, the opposite is often the case. Many teachers unwittingly create situations in which student failure is virtually inevitable. This may be the result of poor organisation, unrealistic aims and objectives, confusing explanations, fuzzy instructions, trying to fit too much into the one lesson, and so on.

These negative situations will undermine student confidence and may even reinforce failure. So avoid them at all costs.

CREATIVE VISUALISATION: USING THE IMAGINATION TO CREATE SUCCESS

Creative visualisation can be used for many reasons: to increase winning chances, for shyness, stress, coping with illness and even everyday situations. Most people possess a great deal of imaginative potential which is never used.

The positive power of imagery and imagination can be useful in the classroom, providing that the students are in a relaxed mood, and the goals are realistic and clearly defined. The teacher must be well informed about the subject, and the student happy and enthusiastic about what they are going to learn during the lesson. Most importantly, they need to believe that when a process has been achieved, they can then proceed to more advanced projects.

To practise creative visualisation, we are not suggesting that you study psychology, or put your students to sleep with your hypnotic voice. We do suggest, however, that you experiment with the techniques outlined below to motivate students and improve their performance.

Examine the following examples and decide whether they could be adapted to develop creative visualisation ideas for your craft classes. The felt-making example below is somewhat different to the usual crafts, but it is fascinating and effective nevertheless.

When the students are settled and you have their attention, you could ask them to relax, close their eyes, get comfortable and take several deep breaths.

Picture a small village in Iran. The buildings are low, made from mud bricks. A pine tree grows nearby, its bark rubbed smooth from climbing feet and the leaning backs of children, sorting shorn wool into piles of various colours. Pots of steaming water stand in the corner. Other pots are water chilled. Men with skull-capped hats and baggy trousers, are felting today, making warm coats for those out shepherding flocks in wind and snow. The women chatter while they chop behind the walls. The felter is seated with his mallet and bow. The gut vibrating makes the wool fluffier for the layered process of felting.

Today we are going to make a sample felt square. The wool you have carded will be in three layers, each placed in an opposite direction on your old sheeting, and stitched down with long running stitches. The ends of the sheet are folded in and stitched. The square is tightly rolled around your small dowel stick and held on with rubber bands.

Wearing rubber gloves, place this bundle alternately in hot and cold water. The bundle is then washed with soap and beaten up and down and around and around. Unwrap the bundle and turn it in the other direction. Feel the wool felt, the fibres beginning to harden. Repeat the soap and water process, then the beating. Unwrap and check for felting. Remove the water, iron, trim, and there is enough felt for a small tea cosy or placemat.

The next example presents a creative visualisation for the popular craft of découpage. It sets up romantic, visual images in the students' minds which will prepare them for the task ahead.

Take yourself back in history to eighteenth century France, to the court of the young queen Marie Antoinette and her ladies-in-waiting as they pass autumn days at the splendid palace of Versailles. The summer has been spent in the gardens, playing at being 'peasants' in the little hamlet the Queen has had built for her make-

believe pastoral games. But now the weather has grown cooler. Marie Antoinette and her courtiers have gathered in the Queen's drawing room, all decorated in her favourite colours of white and gold, to pursue the latest craze of the autumn season at court: découpage.

The ladies are cheerfully cutting up pictures to decorate and glue onto fans and boxes. The pictures may be of idyllic rural scenes, Rococo cherubs, cornucopias of fruit or lavish bouquets and baskets of flowers. But these are not just any pictures; the ladies are cutting up genuine paintings by Watteau, Boucher and Fragonard to satisfy their craze for découpage. Later the Queen will have the fans and boxes sent off to master artisans who will varnish them according to a traditional formula passed from one generation of artisans to the next.

Today we are going to use the same kind of source material as the Queen herself, but our paintings will be reproduction Watteaus, Bouchers and Fragonards, cut from the art books and prints we have been collecting for this workshop. Using these Rococo images, you will cut and compose an arrangement of pictures which pleases you. The motifs will be sealed and then glued onto a wooden box. Later you will sink and preserve your work under many layers of varnish. The result will be an heirloom to treasure always.

BOOSTING SELF CONFIDENCE THROUGH POSITIVE REINFORCEMENT

Positive reinforcement involves rewarding your students for work well done. This is as vital with adults as it is with children.

It can be as simple as a few words of praise. You might say something like: 'I think that's the best yet' or 'That's great! Well done'. Or it could be holding up a student's work for approbation by the class. It can also take the form of actual rewards — little prizes, 'freebies', samples, even jellybeans or stickers! This may sound corny, but adults love it. It is wise, however, to ensure that everybody has received a prize by the end of the course/workshop.

Take your camera along to class and photograph the students' masterpieces in progress and later the finished efforts. Keep the photographs in a special album. One teacher who does this, says:

> *At the end of every workshop, I ask students to pose with their projects for a class photograph. I put the photos in a special keepsakes album of which I am very proud. I know this makes my students feel special.*

A formalised type of positive reinforcement is to present a certificate of achievement at the end of the course. For teachers in a TAFE or similar situation, certificates may be awarded by the institution. If you teach more informally, there is no reason why your students shouldn't be rewarded too. Make certificates from coloured Canson paper, available from art suppliers.

It is the kind of paper calligraphers use. Cut the paper to A4 size or another standard size which will fit a photocopier. To design the certificate, type the wording, print it on a word processor or use commercial pressed type lettering and borders from the newsagent. Once the master copy is prepared, it can be photocopied onto the coloured paper. Write in the names with a calligraphy pen, roll the certificates and tie with a ribbon. Certificates could be presented at an end-of-course get-together.

Another excellent source of positive reinforcement is to organise an exhibition and possibly a sale of students' work. The ideal time to hold an exhibition is in the month or so prior to Christmas. Consider a champagne opening for your students' families and friends. Such events are wonderful confidence boosters for even the shyest and most insecure members of the class.

CHECKLIST FOR MOTIVATION
- Create successful situations.
- Praise your students.
- Believe in them.
- Inspire them.
- Exhibit their work.
- Photograph their masterpieces.
- Present prizes and certificates.

COPING WITH DIFFICULT AND SPECIAL NEEDS STUDENTS

In the craft classroom you will encounter all kinds of personalities. Some students' behaviour undermines the harmony of the group. Other students may have special needs which require a different teaching approach.

Who are they and what can you do about them?

THE LATECOMER

Latecomers are usually upset and apologetic and may well have a genuine excuse. Reassure them and tell them not to rush. Do not allow their lateness and panic to disrupt the group.

As mentioned earlier, only you can decide how long to wait for latecomers. A late student must accept that the teacher cannot just stop the lesson and repeat what they have missed. Spend a few extra minutes with this student when time permits.

Lateness seems to be a particular problem for home studios (page 55), and you need to state your expectations from the very first lesson. Common courtesy dictates that, no matter where a class is held, students should arrive on time, and preferably a few minutes before the scheduled start so that they can unpack and be ready to start on time.

THE DEMANDER

This student wants to monopolise your attention. Demanders are often poor listeners. They interrupt frequently, usually asking you to repeat something which everyone else has already grasped. Be firm here. Remind them you will get to them in turn. In the meantime, they could go over their notes, or perhaps continue with some work they have already mastered.

THE STUDENT WHO NEVER HAS ENOUGH

The Student Who Never Has Enough is enthusiastic but, like the Demander, tries to dominate the teacher's time. Often through keenness rather than bad manners, they will chat on to the teacher, unmindful of the fact that the lesson has finished some time ago and the teacher wants to go home.

Again, be firm but polite. While commending their enthusiasm, explain that you have to leave, the lesson has ended but you appreciate their feedback and comments.

FRIENDS CHATTING

This can be a real problem, especially if you are demonstrating or explaining a point. Try not to be sarcastic and do not attempt to speak over them. Stop the lesson, wait, don't speak. Let their chatter be heard by all. If necessary, suggest nicely that they wait till coffee break to continue. If you don't want to confront them as such, try this teacher's trick:

> *If students are chatting and distracting me and the class,*
> *I speed up the pace of the lesson for a time (or give them*
> *extra work to do). They are so busy keeping up they don't*
> *have time to chatter.*

THE KNOW-IT-ALL

The Know-It-All can undermine your own self confidence, particularly if you are a novice teacher or lacking in confidence yourself. Smile sweetly and thank the Know-It-All for sharing their knowledge with the class. Throw their comments over to the class — there may be someone smarter! Ask the Know-It-All some questions. If they really are smart, use them as a resource and don't be intimidated by them.

THE INSECURE STUDENT WHO IS OUT OF THEIR DEPTH

Insecure Students need jollying along. Try to build up their confidence but do not allow them to take up too much class time. Use positive reinforcement and praise (see page 41) to boost self esteem. Joke that you don't wake up in the morning and know it all. Assure them that with practice, we can all be competent crafters. Tell a joke on yourself. Describe your first attempt.

A doll-making teacher suggests this strategy:

> *When I encounter an insecure student, I ask her a little*
> *about herself. Often she is a very competent cook or gardener*
> *or whatever, and I tell her that we are just going to channel*
> *a little bit of that expertise into her doll-making.*

THE PANICKER

There is usually a Panicker in every class. Sometimes the Panicker and the Latecomer are one in the same. They arrive flustered and seem to be accident prone. There is always some crisis happening to them. Don't let them disrupt the other members of the class. Surprisingly enough, they are often excellent crafters and will amaze you at the end of the lesson by producing something really good. These people seem to be panicky by nature — perhaps it gets their adrenalin going. Try not to be unnerved by them.

THE ARGUER/ CHALLENGER

This student can be a real problem. Try to avoid a personality clash. Arguers and Challengers feel they have to assert their superiority over you, the teacher. Don't take it personally. They may have a permanent chip on their shoulder. You cannot let them get under your skin. Grit your teeth. Smile. They may well hold high qualifications and, if so, will certainly let you know about them. Do not be put down. Call their bluff. Give them more work to do. Or, with their permission, show their work to the class for comment. Remember you are in charge: 'One ship — one captain'.

THE SIDETRACKER/RAMBLER

Like the Student Who Never Has Enough, these students are well-meaning, kind and often in need of social contact. They tend to regale the class with lengthy anecdotes which will lead the class away from the task at hand, particularly if you are demonstrating or explaining a point. Respond briefly and politely. Tactfully cut short any long story-telling and then get right back to work.

THE SILENT PARTICIPANT

These students are not a disruptive influence on the class. Quite the opposite. You hardly know they are there and they tend to be ignored. It is important to help these reticent members of the class feel comfortable and to give them their fair share of attention.

THE SILENT SUFFERER

The Silent Sufferers may not have understood but are too polite or shy to make their problem known. The only way to identify a Silent Sufferer is to circulate around the class, looking for problems. The active, alert teacher will soon identify and help a Silent Sufferer.

THE SICK STUDENT

The Sick Student is not a discipline problem but a problem nevertheless. If the situation is an emergency, seek the help of those in charge of the shop or institution. Often, among the students, there is someone with some first aid knowledge. If the situation is serious and distressing, then the class should be cancelled. For other sickness, suggest that the student rest somewhere quiet, or phone relatives or friends to come and pick him or her up. It is worthwhile checking if there are any first aid facilities at the venue, particularly when working with elderly people.

THE SPECIAL NEEDS STUDENT

You may have to use lateral thinking to develop techniques to assist the Special Needs Student. He or she may be hearing or sight impaired, or have another physical handicap which makes doing craft difficult. As teacher, you need to come up with ways and means of making your craft accessible to these students.

For hearing impaired students, make your presentation visual: lots of demonstrations, diagrams and notes on the board. Remember, that if the student has lip reading skills, you must face the student when speaking. It is easy to forget and start speaking from behind the student or at a board with your back turned.

For sight impaired students, magnifiers or combined magnifying glass and light may be useful. If you have a computer, consider printing class notes in a larger point size. Alternatively, have them enlarged on a photocopier. The elderly also appreciate enlarged type.

Choose projects which are suited to your students. A student who is sight impaired or arthritic may not be able to attempt an intricate cross-stitch but could well succeed at longstitch. In all crafts, avoid small fiddly items and try to work on large, flat surfaces. The really seriously handicapped person usually requires specialised teaching, almost one to one.

A special group whom right-handed teachers often forget is the left-handed student. Teachers tend to let them work things out for themselves. However, if you sit in front of a left-hander and demonstrate, this acts as a mirror. Similarly, it is a good idea to have a mirror on hand, when teaching a technique side by side to a left-hander.

Foreign language speakers with little or no English can also be viewed as having special needs. In her decorative painting classes, Deborah has taught a number of Japanese students with no English at all:

> *Because of my background as a language teacher, I recognise the importance of presenting lots of visual cues to my students. I work from an easel as well as going around to each student and showing them individually. It is amazing how much can be communicated through visual presentation, plus mime and gestures, particularly when the students are so enthusiastic about learning.*

CHECKLIST FOR COPING WITH DIFFICULT SITUATIONS

- Be patient.
- Take control.
- Be observant.
- Keep your sense of humour.
- Remain calm.
- Be flexible.
- Be firm but polite.
- 'One ship — one captain'.

EVALUATING THE LESSON

SELF ASSESSMENT AND FEEDBACK

Continual self assessment and evaluation is another important aspect of teaching arts and crafts. Not only do you have to be prepared to make a quick evaluation in class and act on it, but you also need to take stock of your success or otherwise at the end of a lesson or course.

Although a good teacher often intuitively knows when to make a change and for what reason, he or she should also welcome feedback from other sources. If there should be comments and or criticism, an open mind is needed, followed by appropriate action.

If you are not receiving feedback, then you could ask direct questions: 'Did you like the fabric painting today? Did you learn something new? Do you think you could do this on your own now?'

If your students tell you they really enjoyed the lesson, this is positive feedback, and you both feel good. On the other hand, another student might say: 'I found that very difficult. I don't think I'll ever be any good at this.' Such negative feedback requires further investigation. The comment may not necessarily reflect the quality of teaching. Some outside factors may have influenced this student. You could ask: 'Why did you find the task difficult?' The answer might surprise you. The student may have been tired, doubts if she can manage, now wishes she had gone to another class, etc.

Some teachers are apprehensive about seeking comments on their teaching but have been pleasantly surprised:

> *I was scared at first to ask students to fill out the questionnaire the college gave me to distribute at the end of the course. But the comments were generally good and I was encouraged. There were one or two things that needed changing, particularly towards the end of the course where I was not aware that I crammed in too much work, causing the class to panic.*

If you are receiving a lot of negative feedback — for instance, students are dropping out or changing to other classes, you need to examine your whole approach to teaching. Take note of your body language and the tone of your voice. Are you approachable, greeting questions with a smile, or are you intimidating? Are your directions clear? Are your projects too easy, too hard, unappealing?

Learning is a shared process between teacher and student. In class, allow time for exchange of ideas, information and questions. The negative aspects may have shown up earlier, had you asked more questions.

SELF EVALUATION FOR THE CRAFT TEACHER

Rate yourself on these teaching skills by circling a number between 1 and 5. 1 = Excellent, 3 = Fair, 5 = Poor.

Excellent		Fair		Poor
1	2	3	4	5

PREPARATION OF LESSON

- Preparation of class notes, pattern, instructions, etc.   1 2 3 4 5
- Gauging correct level of difficulty of teaching material.   1 2 3 4 5
- Estimating appropriate time required for the task.   1 2 3 4 5
- Identifying skills to be taught.   1 2 3 4 5
- Choosing situations and tasks in which the student, at his or her current level of ability, will succeed.   1 2 3 4 5
- Preparation of teaching aids.   1 2 3 4 5

STARTING THE LESSON

- Starting the lesson in a positive way.   1 2 3 4 5
- Focussing students on the task at hand.   1 2 3 4 5
- Relaxing the class.   1 2 3 4 5
- Knowing and using students' names.   1 2 3 4 5

TEACHING TECHNIQUES

- Presenting a warm and friendly personality.   1 2 3 4 5
- Coping with difficult students.   1 2 3 4 5
- Explaining material clearly.   1 2 3 4 5
- Asking pertinent questions.   1 2 3 4 5
- Awareness of lack of understanding of your instructions and taking steps to remedy this.   1 2 3 4 5

- Pacing the lesson well so that students do not
  become bored but, at the same time, are not rushed.   1 2 3 4 5
- Using a wide range of teaching techniques and strategies. 1 2 3 4 5
- Using practical examples, related anecdotes, humour.   1 2 3 4 5
- Encouraging students to be flexible and creative.   1 2 3 4 5
- Offering constructive criticism.   1 2 3 4 5
- Helping students to evaluate their own work.   1 2 3 4 5
- Revising work already done.   1 2 3 4 5
- Closing the lesson in an organised way.   1 2 3 4 5

MOTIVATING STUDENTS

- Using positive reinforcement to boost
  students' confidence.   1 2 3 4 5
- Keeping the better students occupied and challenged.   1 2 3 4 5
- Assisting the weaker students without allowing
  them to monopolise your time.   1 2 3 4 5

REVIEW AND EVALUATION

- Evaluating your teaching style and techniques
  and the success of your lesson.   1 2 3 4 5
- Seeking feedback from students and employer.   1 2 3 4 5

PROFESSIONALISM AND PRACTICALITIES

- Being on time to class.   1 2 3 4 5
- Keeping professional confidences.   1 2 3 4 5
- Observing copyright ethics.   1 2 3 4 5
- Sharing knowledge freely.   1 2 3 4 5
- Organising class supplies well ahead of class.   1 2 3 4 5
- Keeping records and copies of class notes
  to be used again.   1 2 3 4 5
- Keeping records of your receipts and expenses.   1 2 3 4 5

HOW DID YOU SCORE?

TOTAL	STANDARD	SUMMARY
All '1's	Excellent	A perfect score. What more can we do or say to help you? You know it all. Maintaining this extremely high teaching standard requires a lot of hard work on your part to remain the best. Congratulations.
Mainly '1's and '2's	Very high	Excellent, too. Keep up this high standard; you are in the top range of teachers.
Mainly '2's	Very good	Great result. Who wants to be perfect? Most teachers feel comfortable in this range.
'2's and '3's	Good	A good teaching score. There are some areas where you can improve. Work through the '3's.
Mainly '3's	Average	You are honest. Possibly you have not been teaching long. Work through the most important areas, such as lesson planning, first. You may need some seminar assistance.
Mainly '4's and '5's	Below Average	Take heart. You may have been thrown in at the deep end. Do you need to update your craft skills? Re-read the book and improve your weakest areas first. Attend teaching seminars.

RUNNING CLASSES AT HOME

HOME TEACHING CONSIDERATIONS

Teaching at home is an ideal way of sharing a love and knowledge of your craft with others, while at the same time being close to your family and making some money. It has the advantages that times can be organised to suit yourself, you do not have to travel, nor do you have to share your earnings with a shop or other institution. The home teacher has complete control over the teaching situation. In addition, there is nothing quite like the friendly, relaxed atmosphere that is part of teaching at home.

> *I would never teach anywhere but at home. My time is my own; I arrange my schedule around my family. I charge reasonable fees and have no need to advertise. I am happy and have no desire to expand my horizons.*

Home teaching is particularly suited to young mothers who would like to conduct a part-time business but do not want to be away from their children. Needlecrafter, Suzie Roberts of Lilli Pilli, NSW, has conducted a very successful home teaching business for many years. Suzie says it is important to sort out your priorities:

> *My family commitments come first, and I receive total support from my family. I never run classes during school holidays so I can spend that time with the children.*

Others find home teaching too arduous:

> *I always seem to be exhausted. I have to clean the house the day before the class, then do it again after the students have left.*

There are a number of practical issues to consider when teaching from home. For instance, you may need to have the permission of the local council to run a home studio. Generally, councils are quite lenient about home craft studios, as long as class numbers are small, parking is adequate and neighbours do not complain. Sometimes councils will want to inspect the studio to verify it meets fire safety standards, particularly if it is located on an upper floor.

Check with your insurance company to ensure that you have sufficient public liability cover and whether your craft business is covered in your general policy. To be fully protected, you may need to take out an additional policy.

CREATING RULES FOR THE HOME STUDIO

You will also have the responsibility of creating rules and regulations for your classes, just as a craft shop owner would do. Indeed, the teacher at home needs to be even more businesslike and organised because the casual atmosphere of the home studio can foster laxness in the teacher and bad manners in the student.

Some students will take advantage of the fact that you run classes at home and will arrive late, linger after finishing time, bring their babies and toddlers, and so on.

If you teach at home, you must insist on punctuality and respect for your professionalism. Set and state your policies firmly at the outset. Be diplomatic but make sure that students are aware of your expectations.

If students straggle into class late, or talk constantly amongst themselves, remind them tactfully that this behaviour would not be accepted in a school, college or shop situation and is certainly not appropriate in your studio. If you do not want people bringing children to class, state this most firmly from the very first lesson. After all, you are not running a child minding centre.

When I first taught from home, many of my students were mothers with young children. They were often unable to find babysitters and brought their children with them. My home was not suitable for little children and we were all on edge. I have a firm rule now that there are no children.

SETTING UP A HOME STUDIO

Many people begin teaching from their kitchen or dining room table. This situation generally works well for 4 to 6 people, as long as they are not cramped. The available space will dictate class size.

Of course, the ideal situation is a separate studio, but a garage or sunroom can be suitable, particularly if there is a separate entrance and separate or nearby toilet facilities. If students are traipsing through your house to reach the bathroom, this can be disruptive to family members.

A Sydney teacher describes an effective teaching area she has created in her garage:

> *I have a double garage with fluorescent lighting, power points and an old refrigerator. One side of the garage is permanently set up for my classes. I have covered an old table tennis table with black plastic to serve as a work area. The walls are decorated with craft posters and samples of my work. I take out a kettle and tea, coffee, biscuits, etc. There is an outside toilet so students do not have come into the house at all. Originally I advertised for students but now my students keep coming back term after term.*

Once you have set aside a teaching space, try to keep all equipment and supplies together there, with a strictly 'hands-off' policy for the family. If the table has to be cleared after each lesson, at least set up a cupboard or set of shelves nearby which is reserved for your teaching alone.

It is also important to think about lighting, ventilation, furniture, fire safety etc. These issues are covered on pages 6-10.

If you are not in a position to run classes from home but still want to teach independently, hiring a nearby hall or renting space in a shop may be a cost effective alternative:

> *I rented the local scout hall for a morning each week. I was happy for mothers to bring their children, who played at one end of the hall while we worked at the other end. It was chaotic but good fun.*

FEES AND ATTENDANCE

Be professional about arrangements for paying. Again, set out your policies and any special conditions at enrolment time and preferably in writing. This will avoid problems and conflict later.

Classes held at home generally last 2 to 3 hours and are run weekly. Many teachers run a block of lessons, often 6 to ten weeks coinciding with a school semester. Once you have decided on the fee per student per lesson, calculate the total charge for the semester.

Some teachers require a deposit in advance to reserve a place in the class. Usually this deposit is non-refundable, but you must state this on the enrolment form. We suggest you ask for full payment for the course or semester on or before the first lesson. Most teachers will not refund class fees if a student misses a lesson or drops out. However, teachers sometimes make up missed lessons under certain circumstances. Absence owing to sickness might qualify, but if the student takes the morning off to have her hair done, the teacher might not be so sympathetic. If all these conditions are sorted out and in writing, your students know where they stand from day one.

One teacher describes her problems with fees and attendance:

> *I'm a softie. At first I only charged the students when they were here. Some days no-one turned up. I thought they should make a commitment to the craft, so I asked for payment in advance. Attendance improved after that.*

KEEPING RECORDS

Issue receipts when students pay their fees and retain copies. Record these fees in an exercise book or ledger. For more information see 'Taxation Issues', page 70.

It is also important to keep names, addresses and phone numbers of students. These should be recorded on student enrolment forms.

Here is a sample enrolment form:

CONDITIONS OF ENROLMENT
Please read carefully and sign form.

No refunds will be given unless the course is cancelled.

Classes will be cancelled unless a minimum number of six students is enrolled in the course.

Refunds are not given for missed classes or if the semester is not completed. In the event that the teacher is ill, classes will be made up.

Fees must be paid before students can attend classes.

A deposit of 50% of class fee is required to secure a place in the class, balance to be paid when or before the class commences.

NAME:
ADDRESS:
PHONE (Home and Work):
CLASS/WORKSHOP:
SIGNATURE:

Not only is this information essential if you have to contact students urgently, but it also serves as the basis of a mailing list for marketing future classes (see later section). If you have a personal computer, consider typing in this information to create a data base for a mailing list.

PROVIDING SUPPLIES

When students enrol, provide a list of supplies. See page 25. If you have a registered business, you will be able to order products wholesale and sell them back to your students at a profit. Most home teachers, however, do not qualify as wholesale purchasers and cannot make any real profit from selling supplies to their students.

Nevertheless, they may want to provide materials as a convenient service for their students. You could cut costs by ordering certain items in bulk and then pass on the savings to students or take a small profit for yourself.

You could also suggest to a local craft shop that you will order class supplies through them if they offer you a discount. Ten to fifteen percent is customary. You can then supply your students and cover the cost of your time and petrol in obtaining the materials. If you do not want to supply the products yourself, approach the shop and offer to refer your students, if the craft store agrees to give them a discount. If you can guarantee steady sales to the shop, they may even order in special materials for you, but make sure you give plenty of notice.

Although the relationship between home teachers and shop owners is usually harmonious and mutually profitable, there are exceptions. This shop owner complains:

> *I have lost many of my students to home studios. I resent the fact that home teachers can undercut me by charging lower class fees because they have no overheads.*

MARKETING YOUR CLASSES

If you teach in a shop, school or evening college, the marketing of your classes will be largely done by the proprietors or administrators. Even so, the best marketing tool is 'word of mouth'. Your reputation as a fine teacher is the best way to sell classes and to have students return year after year. But, by the same token, remember that negative word of mouth can be fatal.

If you have established a good relationship with the local craft store and your classes do not overlap with any that they run, the proprietor may be prepared to pass on your name to customers who enquire about classes. On a more formal basis, you could have your business cards or class flyers on display for interested customers. The shop owner may even agree to display your class pieces. This is to his or her advantage as well, because they can then show finished samples using the products they sell.

Enquire about placing flyers or posters advertising your classes at the local library, community centre, playgroup, school and so on. Make this promotional material simple and eye-catching. Calligraphers could hand-letter their flyers. Folk artists might add a painted motif. Other craftspeople could design an appropriate logo which will attract attention. Flyers look attractive when photocopied on coloured paper.

As discussed earlier, use previous class lists to formulate a mailing list. Send out class information to former students and they may well return to the fold. Suggest that they bring a friend. You could even organise a special free 'bring a friend' class so prospective students could sample your craft.

Displays and exhibitions at your studio, 'open house' parties and craft morning teas are all good ways of attracting new students. Have class samples for next semester on display, plus examples of students' work. Give a brief demonstration of your craft. Demonstrations create tremendous interest. Enrolment forms should be on hand so that interested visitors can sign up for classes.

Advertisements in the classified section of the local newspaper are also effective in letting people know about your classes. Many newspapers run regular 'Crafts' pages which accept advertising and run feature articles on local craftspeople. Note that they are more likely to do an article about you if you advertise with them.

Act as your own public relations consultant and send the paper a 'press release' about yourself. It should be about four or five paragraphs, neatly typed and written in the third person:

> *Sally Bloggs, embroidery teacher of Sydney, recently won First Prize at the Royal Easter Show for her grub rose embroidered cushion. Sally teaches her award-winning needlecraft skills at her home studio, 20 Waratah Street.*

Try to include an 'angle' in your press release. In the press release above, the 'angle' is winning a prestigious award. But it might also be that your craft is an unusual one; you may have been involved in a craft service project for charity; there might be an interesting student in the class — very old or very young, and so on. Include a black and white photograph of yourself at work. If the paper is really impressed, they will send out a photographer and perhaps a journalist to interview you.

Consider the timing of any promotional activity you organise. In September or October, leading up to Christmas, is a great time to advertise Christmas craft classes. Just before the start of a new semester, particularly the start of the school year is also ideal. January is a time when people, inspired by New Year's resolutions to take up a new activity, are looking around for courses to do. So take advantage of this burst of enthusiasm.

CHECKLIST FOR THE HOME STUDIO
- Check insurance, council regulations, fire safety.
- Advertise.
- Set up teaching space.
- Put up 'Rules'.
- Clean house/Do not clean house!
- Have students complete enrolment forms.
- Collect fees and keep receipts.

TEACHING THROUGH SHOPS AND STUDIOS

Many of the issues which may arise when dealing with shops and studios have been covered in 'The Ethical Teacher', page 12, 'Establishing Fees', page 16, and other sections of the book.

ESTABLISHING CREDENTIALS

When approaching shops and studios for teaching work, present yourself in a professional manner. Take along samples of your work. Start a portfolio containing photographs of your work. Include some of your lesson handouts and any other relevant material. You could also prepare a short biography or curriculum vitae, listing your craft interests and achievements, the craft courses you have attended, membership of craft associations and details of any previous teaching you have done. Include names of referees and their positions.

SETTLING FINANCIAL MATTERS

It cannot be repeated too often that you should sort out financial matters at the start. In discussing these matters, try to cover every conceivable eventuality:

- Rate of pay.
- Method of payment.
- When you are paid.
- Are fees calculated by class size?
- Or is there a flat rate?
- Will you be paid a cancellation fee if the shop cancels the class?
- Who pays for photocopying?
- Is there a teacher discount for purchases made at the shop?

If the shop asks you to prepare a sample piece, establish who owns the sample. To avoid ambiguity, purchase the project piece yourself (at teacher's discount) and lend it back to the shop for display.

THE SHOP OWNER'S EXPECTATIONS

Another potential source of disharmony is conflicting expectations as to the goals of the craft class. Just as the goals of the course should be discussed with your students, you also need to do the same with the shop proprietor. As an artisan, you may perceive your aims in a rather more philosophical way than the shop owner. You are there to share a love of craft, to teach skills, to foster creativity in your students. The shop proprietor, naturally enough, has more down-to-earth, commercial concerns on his or her mind. Sometimes the two different mind sets are incompatible.

The shop owner may want you to teach a new project every week. After all, it is in his or her interest to sell more products. You, on the other hand, want to spend some time reinforcing the skills you are teaching, rather than rushing helter skelter from one project to the next. You may see your major commitment as being to your students, but you also need to appreciate the shop owner's position. The bottom line is that he or she is paying you!

Remember the shop proprietor is not 'the enemy', quite the contrary. If he or she did not try to run a successful commercial venture, you might be out of a job. Try to reach a compromise between the two positions.

> *The shop owner wanted me to teach four beginners' projects in four weeks. The students and I were exhausted. We didn't have time to cover the basics and students were not well enough prepared to move onto the next level. I discussed this with the owner and we have now extended the beginners' course to six weeks.*

Yet another problem is that shop owners will sometimes place novice students in intermediate or advanced classes. One student comments:

> *Teachers need to be aware that certain craft shop owners book students into classes which are beyond their level of ability. I admired a pretty floral project, explained I was a beginner and asked the shop owner if she thought I could cope in the class. Her answer was: 'Yes, of course you could do it.' Fortunately I ran into the teacher before I actually booked for the class. When I asked her about it, she told me there was no way I could cope at my current level of expertise, and that I should do some more basic lessons first.*

A teacher comments:

> *I feel sorry for students who are just put in to fill up the class, especially beginners, when the class and project have been prepared for advanced students. It is unfair to everybody.*

Ensure that the proprietor is aware of the level of ability required and that your pre-class information clearly states this. Be specific: list the skills the student should have mastered before attempting this project. Then, both shop owner and student will know exactly what is required.

It may be in the shop owner's immediate interests to book a student of inappropriate ability into a class in order to build up class numbers. However, in the long run, such action will only damage his or her business and cause conflict with teachers and students.

Remember, however, that no matter how well you think you have covered this matter, there will always be students who book into classes way beyond their ability. They will usually leave the class, feeling frustrated. They may even blame you for their failure! But if they have been fully informed of the prerequisites beforehand, you have covered yourself and should accept no blame.

LIAISING WITH THE SHOP

Organise dates and times for classes well in advance, and if possible, confirm them in writing. Just a short note or fax will do. Then, if there has been an error or misunderstanding on either side, it can be remedied early.

It is vital to supply the shop with a list of requirements as early as possible. Similarly, you will need to prepare pre-class information for the students. See pages 25-6.

Clarify the shop's policy on students using their own supplies. Most craft shops insist that students purchase the major items for the project, such as fabric, clay, glass, paper, canvas, greenware or a wood piece at the shop itself. Because shop owners often put very little mark-up on class fees, their profit lies in selling products. If students purchased their major supplies for the class elsewhere, then classes would soon become unprofitable to run.

Phone the shop a couple of days prior to the class or workshop to confirm that stock has arrived, to obtain numbers and names and to organise any special equipment or teaching aids. If it is your first visit, check on the location and where to park. Enquire about the time the shop owner will arrive to open up. You do not want to be sitting out on the footpath for an hour waiting to get in!

Liaising works both ways. An efficient shop owner should let you know if there have been any last minute changes. This teacher voices a common complaint:

> *Nothing annoys me more. I prepare for ten students and the shop puts in two extra at the last minute and doesn't tell me. This takes up precious time as no preparation has been done for these extra students and the class is held up.*

A POSITIVE CASE STUDY: FANTASY MARBLE FINISH WORKSHOP

What actually happens when a workshop is planned and run at a craft shop or studio? Here is a possible scenario, viewed from three points of view: the shop, the teacher and the student.

The shop was approached by a popular teacher in the area about introducing new skills into their workshops. The teacher's specialty was faux finishes. The shop was equally keen to run a workshop in faux finishes as they stocked a range of decorator paints and wanted to promote crafts that used home decorating products.

THE SHOP'S POINT OF VIEW

The project chosen was a stool, suitable for beginners. The teacher was asked to paint a sample stool for display in the shop to promote the workshop. The teacher purchased the stool through the shop at teacher's discount as she intended to keep it herself to teach at other venues.

When the date of the workshop had been set, the shop proprietor calculated the cost. The workshop was aimed at beginners who would probably have little or no equipment, so a kit of basic materials would be included in the fee.

The next task was to enrol the students, through displaying the sample stool in the shop, advertising in the local paper, phone calls and mailing list. The shop owner commented:

> I use a mailing list built up over many years, and most importantly, personal contact with my customers. Word of mouth is an excellent way to promote workshops.
>
> Notifying and telephoning students can be an awful job. They are always out and never return calls. Before workshops I have one staff member almost continually phoning people. Then they say they are coming and don't. Some promise to send deposits and forget. I now keep waiting lists and insist on full payment before the workshop.

After eight weeks' promotion by the shop, the workshop was fully booked, with full payment received from each student, the fee being non-refundable in the event of cancellation, unless the place could be filled by someone else.

Students had been sent or given their requirements lists for the workshop. Stools had been ordered and were now in the shop. Kits were ready, placed in plastic bags, each labelled with the student's name.

On the day of the class, the shop owner ensured that there were tea and coffee making supplies on hand. She greeted each student and directed them to the teaching area of the shop where the teacher awaited their arrival.

THE TEACHER'S POINT OF VIEW

Having had the details of the workshop (project, dates and fees) confirmed, the teacher painted the sample stool that same week and took it to the shop, together with a list of the items required for the beginners' kit and a printed requirements list for the students. This gave the shop plenty of time to promote the class, order in materials and organise bookings.

Here is the pre-class sheet the teacher prepared for the students:

FANTASY FAUX MARBLE WORKSHOP
WITH JANE ROSE

at 'Furniture avec une difference',
25 Oak Street, French's Forest, opposite the Post Office,
on Saturday, August 9
from 10 am sharp to 4 pm.

In this beginners' workshop, we will be creating a
fantasy marble finish on a wooden stool. You will be
able to adapt the techniques you learn in class to a
wide range of home decorating uses.
You will receive your stool and a complete beginners'
kit of materials on the day. All you need to bring with
you is:

- *your lunch*
- *a mug*
- *an apron*
- *a notebook and pen*

I look forward to seeing you on 9th August.
Be prepared to have fun.

Jane

The teacher composed a personal reminder list and schedule for the workshop:

- *Venue: 'Furniture avec une difference', Oak Street, French's Forest.*
- *Phone: 968 4529.*
- *Date: Saturday, 9th August.*
- *Times: 10 am to 4 pm.*
- *Reminders: Take icecream containers, plastic plates, gloves, sponge, paper towels, apron, notes, sample boards, corkboard, paints, brushes, feathers, photo album, camera, lunch. Phone on Friday, 8th August for names.*
- *Leave home 8.30 to allow one hour for travelling. Set up from 9.30 am.*

The teacher's actual schedule for teaching this workshop appears in 'Pacing The Lesson', page 36.

THE STUDENT'S POINT OF VIEW

The student saw an advertisement for the faux marble workshop in the local newspaper and phoned to enquire about details. After visiting the shop and viewing the sample, she enrolled and paid the required amount. She completed and signed a form which stated the conditions of enrolment and explained the shop's policy on refunds. A sheet of information about the workshop was given to her, and, as a beginner with no knowledge of the craft, she was pleased to see that all materials were included in the cost.

She arrived at quarter to ten on the morning of the workshop and went into the teaching area where a bag of materials with her name on it awaited her. She was warmly welcomed by the teacher who had a name tag ready for her and suggested that she help herself to a pre-class cup of coffee.

A NEGATIVE CASE STUDY

Now let's look at the same workshop but this time, things do not run so efficiently. Indeed, it is more like a nightmare for everyone concerned.

SHOP'S POINT OF VIEW

Basic organisation and costing proceeded as for the first case study. The shop owner decided there was plenty of time to advertise the class, so did not undertake any promotion at this stage. She did not hear from the teacher about supplying the sample stool and was too busy with other things to follow up on this. Eventually the teacher dropped in with the sample stool a few days before the workshop. It was at this time the shop owner realised she had only two names for the class — two regulars to whom she had mentioned the workshop in passing.

She rang her wood supplier to order the stools, only to find that it would be three weeks' before they could supply her. So she had to purchase them at retail from another craft shop which meant that they would cost significantly more than the original estimate.

At their initial meeting the teacher had mentioned the supplies required for the beginners' kit but the shop owner had forgotten the details. She rang the teacher the night before the class and asked what was needed. As it happened, the shop was out of several of the required colours, and others would have to be substituted.

The same evening, the shop owner desperately rang around her regular customers and friends trying to fill the class. She was eventually able to come up with five students. She forgot to tell them the starting time of the class, and next morning one lady arrived at 9 am, a half hour before opening time while several straggled in at 10.15.

The owner had not had time to prepare the beginners' kits, so she told students to come out to the shop area for supplies as required during the day. She had to explain that their stools would not look exactly like the sample because some of the colours were unavailable.

TEACHER'S POINT OF VIEW

After her initial discussions with the shop owner, the teacher decided that there were still two months until the workshop, so there was no need to prepare anything yet. She painted the sample the weekend before the workshop and delivered it to the shop on August 4.

On the morning of the class the teacher had to wait for her husband to return from his early morning golf game. She quickly assembled the materials she thought she would need. She couldn't find any rubber gloves or plastic plates and had to purchase these at the supermarket on the way to the class. This made her late and she didn't reach the shop until just after ten.

STUDENT'S POINT OF VIEW

On Friday evening, August 8, the prospective student was phoned by the shop owner who said that there was a last minute vacancy in a faux finish class the next day and that it was a wonderful opportunity to learn from a well known and highly respected teacher. The student agreed to come and had to quickly organise a babysitter for her two children as her husband worked on Saturdays.

When the student arrived at the shop in the morning, things appeared rather chaotic. The shop owner was pacing anxiously, awaiting the arrival of the teacher. Nobody quite knew what was going on. Finally the teacher arrived, hot and flustered. Some of the students had not yet arrived. The lesson finally commenced at quarter to eleven.

THE AFTERMATH

After the class, the shop owner commented:

> *I doubt if I will ever have that teacher working for me again! She was late, then expected me to do half her work for her. I spent most of Friday evening phoning around for students. There was no profit in the workshop and I am very disappointed.*

Like the shop owner, the teacher blamed everyone but herself:

> *I had bad vibes about this from the beginning. The shop was messy and disorganised. The children slept in that morning and my husband had gone to golf and came back late with the car. The class was upset because there was no pink paint. At least I received a big fat cheque at the end of the day.*

The student was the meat in the sandwich:

> *I was really given the 'hard sell' by the shop. All I wanted was to paint a pink stool for the nursery. But there was only blue paint available. What a day! The teacher was late, I got paint all over my good dress — nobody told me to bring an apron. The teacher hardly came near me all day. She sat up the front gossiping with a couple of the other students about soap operas. They covered every topic except how to paint the stool. My stool now sits unfinished in the garage — a dreadful blue. Never again!*

YOUR CHECKLIST FOR DEALING WITH SHOPS AND STUDIOS
- Be professional at all times.
- Establish your credentials and specify your capabilities.
- State your needs.
- Listen to their needs.
- Settle financial matters at the outset. Be explicit about fees.
- Establish minimum and maximum class numbers.
- Organise and confirm dates and times.
- Provide list of required materials.
- Check stock.
- Check facilities and equipment.
- Establish who owns sample pieces.
- Ascertain the shop's policy on students using their own supplies such as fabrics, wood pieces, etc.
- Phone to obtain numbers and names.

BOOKKEEPING AND TAXATION ISSUES

BOOKKEEPING

There are several simple systems you can use to keep a record of income and expenses. Remember that if you are audited by the Taxation Office you will need to produce these records, so storing receipts in an old shoe box and jotting teaching income on scraps of paper may not be good enough.

Keep a record of all your income from classes. If you teach at several different shops, list the income from each shop separately. If you run a home studio, issue receipts when your students pay their fees, and retain copies.

It is easier to maintain ongoing records than to have to sort out hundreds of receipts at the end of the tax year. One method is to keep a ledger with a record of monthly income and a detailed list of expenses incurred in that month. In the expenses section, for each month, have a column for each category of expense, for example, photocopying, stationery, subscriptions, self-education courses, etc. Staple or pin that month's corresponding receipts together and store them in a clear plastic sleeve or the relevant compartment of a concertina file. If you have a personal computer, you could purchase a simple bookkeeping programme.

TAXATION ISSUES

If you earn money from teaching the occasional class to friends or a church or community group, the Taxation Office may classify this as a hobby and you may not have to declare this income. If you have any doubts, check with an accountant.

If you teach at a shop or run regular classes at home, you will probably need to declare this income to the Taxation Department. Remember that you can be fined for not declaring money you have earned. The Taxation Office has been known to request from craft shops lists of their teachers and craftspeople.

As an artisan/teacher, you can, however, claim a number of deductions. Here are some of the expenses you may be able to claim to reduce your taxable income. Check first with your accountant:

- Craft materials ('tools of trade'). Sometimes these tools of trade can be unusual. Découpeurs purchase expensive art books to cut up for their work, and these are just as much tools of trade as woodworking tools or paints and brushes.

- Teaching aids such as sample boards, videos, slides, easel, cost of photographs, etc.

- Stationery used for teaching and promotional purposes — business cards, folders, name cards, paper, envelopes, plastic sleeves, cardboard, paper clips, staples, etc.

- Photocopying costs.

- Postage and courier costs (when mailing samples and handouts to shops, mailing flyers to students, etc).

- Membership of professional associations.

- Cost of courses undertaken to keep you up-to-date (this can be claimed only if you are teaching now, not intending to teach at some future date). Note also that the first $250 must be deducted from the total amount.

- Registration fees and costs for craft conventions and retreats.

- Cost of relevant reference books.

- Subscriptions to relevant journals and craft magazines.

- Depreciation on professional library, slide collection, major equipment (typewriter, etc.) This involves a complicated mathematical formula — consult your accountant.

- Heating and lighting for your home studio (when used exclusively for painting and lesson preparation — the dining room table doesn't count!)

- Business portion of telephone expenses.

- Any other out-of-pocket expenses related to your teaching.

Under the self assessment system, the onus is on you to keep detailed records. You must retain all receipts in order to substantiate claims. It should be noted that credit card receipts marked 'Goods' will not be accepted by the tax man. The sales assistant must write something specific like 'Art/craft materials'.

Keeping well organised records of income and expenses will ensure that you can face tax time with peace of mind.

USEFUL ADDRESSES

CRAFTS COUNCILS
The Crafts Councils in each state provide information about craft guilds and associations through the Craftline, a nationwide computerised data base. It operates in all Crafts Council offices as a user pays system.

The addresses are:

Crafts Council of Australia, 35 George Street, The Rocks, Sydney, NSW 2000. Phone: (02) 241 1701; Fax (02) 247 6143.

Crafts Council of ACT, 1 Aspinal Street, Watson, ACT 2602. Phone (06) 241 2373.

Crafts Council of NSW, 100 George Street, Sydney, NSW 2000.

Crafts Council of Northern Territory, Conacher Street, Bullocky Point, Darwin, NT 0800. Phone (089) 81 6615.

Crafts Council of Queensland, 166 Ann Street, Brisbane, Qld 4000. Phone: (07) 229 2661.

Crafts Council of South Australia, PO Box 8067, Hindley, SA 5000. Phone (08) 410 1822.

Crafts Council of Tasmania, 11/65 Salamanca Place, Hobart, Tas 7000. Phone: (002) 23 5622.

Crafts Council of Victoria, 114 Gertrude Street, Fitzroy, Vic 3065. Phone: (03) 417 3111.

Crafts Council of Western Australia, 1st Floor, Perth City Railway Station, Wellington Street, Perth, WA 6000. Phone: (09) 325 2799.

COPYRIGHT ADVICE
The Australian Copyright Council, 245 Chalmers Street, Redfern, NSW 2016. Phone: (02) 318 1788.

The Australian Patent, Trademark and Design Office, 189 Kent Street, Sydney, NSW 2000. Phone: (02) 247 9121.

DESIGN
School of Colour and Design, 423 Pacific Highway, Crows Nest, NSW 2065. Phone: (02) 906 4040.

MILNER CRAFT TEACHERS' REGISTER

If you would like to become part of the Milner Craft Teachers' Register and receive news about craft activities, please complete the following form and mail it to:

Sally Milner Publishing Pty Ltd
558 Darling Street, Rozelle, NSW 2039

NAME: _____

ADDRESS: _____

_____

TELEPHONE: (   ) _____

CRAFT TEACHING AREA/S: _____

_____

I would like to receive information about:

☐ Craft teaching seminars.

☐ Craft courses and workshops.

☐ Craft books.

ABOUT THE AUTHORS

Joyce Spencer and Deborah Kneen are both talented craftspeople, sharing wide experience in teaching crafts at community and professional levels.

The fibre crafts have been an interest of Joyce Spencer for many years, and since being introduced to folk and decorative art in the mid '80s, she has developed a passion for faux finishes. She has taught creative weaving at TAFE, as well as community crafts with TAFE Outreach. Joyce has owned a craft shop and teaching studio, and is renowned for the enthusiasm she inspires in her students.

A former high school teacher, Deborah Kneen holds graduate and post-graduate qualifications in education from the University of Sydney. After retiring from school teaching, Deborah became involved in folk art and related crafts. She is the author of two highly successful books on decorative painting and numerous articles in craft magazines. Deborah enjoys teaching all levels of crafters and is noted for her thorough, professional approach.